Louise Durman's Recipes Upon Request

The Most Popular Down-Home Favorites from 10 Years of The News-Sentinel's "Recipes & Requests" Column

 The Knoxville News-Sentinel

Cover illustration and design: Jerry Weintz
Inside illustrations: Charlie Daniel
Back cover photograph: J. Miles Cary
Book layout: Susan Alexander

Contents

▲ ▲ ▲

Foreword: Louise's favorites

In the beginning, "Recipes and Requests" was "Fare for Fair" — a column about the foods people were serving to visitors coming to the World's Fair. The first "Fare," featuring Evelyn McKinney, appeared April 12, 1982. In this collection we include McKinney's recipe for fried peach pies (see page 149) that appeared in that 1982 column.

After the end of the fair, we decided to keep the column because it had become so popular with News-Sentinel readers. In November, 1982, we changed the name to "Recipes and Requests."

Since then we've had many, many nice words from our readers who seem to appreciate the chance to ask for recipes they want and find the answers. Often it's amazing that a long-lost recipe is found.

A reader in 1991, for instance, requested Christmas jam (see page 195), a recipe from Knoxville Utilities Board that appeared years ago. The day the request appeared in The News-Sentinel, a woman called to say that only the day before she had been cleaning out her KUB recipe booklets and had seen the recipe. By the end of that week, three others had responded as well.

So it is with those recipes — enjoyed by a family and shared with News-Sentinel readers — that this cookbook is filled. And it is to all those thoughtful contributors to the "Recipes and Requests" column that this book is dedicated. We have used your names as they appeared with the recipe in The News-Sentinel, and your town, when we knew it.

We know we've missed some of your favorites, but it's impossible to use all the recipes we've been sent over the years. We've added other popular recipes that have appeared in The News-Sentinel, though perhaps not in the "Recipes and Requests" column. We know when a recipe is popular by the number of requests we get for copies of it.

In compiling this book, we resolved to keep a recipe contained on one page for the convenience of the cooks reading it. One space-saving device we use is abbreviations. Though the abbreviations we use are well-known among recipe readers, we'll make doubly sure by listing them here:

lb. is pound

oz. is ounce

qt. is quart

pkg. is package

Tbsp. is tablespoon

tsp. is teaspoon

In addition, any recipe marked with an asterisk (*) is comparatively low in fat and cholesterol.

I wanted to introduce this book with a section of my personal five favorite recipes. That became a nearly impossible task.

How could I pick five? I changed my mind a dozen times. I had at least 12 to begin with, but finally I sprinkled many of the others throughout the book and came up with six favorites starting on the following page:

▲ ▲ ▲
New Year's Eve chili

New Year's Eve chili is so-named because we serve it at New Year's Eve parties with a variety of toppings. Place the toppings in small bowls for guests to select the ones they want. Add tortilla chips or freshly made corn bread. The chili is best when made a day ahead.

3 lbs. choice or lean ground beef

2 large onions, chopped fine

3 to 4 cloves garlic, minced

1 jalapeno pepper, chopped finely or 1 heaping tsp. crushed red pepper

1 tsp. cumin seeds or 2 tsp. ground cumin

1 1/2 Tbsp. oregano

1 Tbsp. sugar (optional, to taste)

6 to 8 Tbsp. chili powder

1 (28-oz.) can whole tomatoes

1 qt. tomato juice

1 (6-oz.) can tomato paste

1 Tbsp. salt

1 tsp. black pepper

2 (16-oz.) cans chili hot beans

8 oz. beer

Saute meat in small amount of oil in skillet until it browns. Remove from skillet and let set on paper towel to absorb fat. Drain most of oil from skillet, leaving only enough to saute onion, garlic and jalapeno pepper until onion is golden. Set aside.

Combine meat with all ingredients in large pot. Bring to a boil, reduce heat and simmer 2 to 3 hours, stirring frequently.

Make a day ahead and refrigerate. Near serving time, skim fat off the top and reheat chili.

Serve with a variety of toppings: shredded cheddar cheese, diced onion, diced green pepper, shredded lettuce. Yield: 6 to 8 servings.

Note: Ground turkey could be used in place of ground beef.

▲ ▲ ▲

Shrimp creole

Shrimp creole is another recipe I like to make for entertaining. Serve it with rice and a layered salad made with a variety of greens and vegetables and a favorite dessert. This creole version came from Charleston, S.C., many years ago.

3 Tbsp. butter or margarine
2 lbs. raw shrimp, shelled and deveined
2 (1 lb.) cans tomatoes
1 (6-oz. can) tomato paste
1 cup chopped onions
1/2 cup chopped green pepper
1 cup chopped celery
2 Tbsp. chopped parsley
3/4 tsp. salt
1/2 tsp. Tabasco sauce
1 bay leaf
1/4 tsp. thyme
1/4 tsp. black pepper
Dash red pepper flakes (optional)
1/2 cup dry white wine
Flour for thickening, if desired

Melt butter in skillet. Add shrimp and saute 2 or 3 minutes, stirring frequently. Remove shrimp from skillet and drain on paper towel.

In large pot, combine ingredients, except shrimp, wine and flour. Bring to boil, reduce heat immediately and simmer 30 minutes. If mixture is thin, stir a little of the hot mixture into about 1/4 cup of flour, stirring to mix well. Return all to pot and stir well. Add shrimp and wine and cook 5 minutes. Remove bay leaf. Serve over hot cooked rice. Yield: 4 to 6 servings.

▲ ▲ ▲

Karen's asparagus quiche

Karen Sproles, owner of the Lunchbox restaurant, Knoxville, makes so many wonderful dishes and we have given many of her recipes in our columns over the years, thanks to her kindness in sharing. But my personal favorite is this apsaragus quiche, made in the springtime when fresh asparagus is in season.

1 (10-inch) pie shell
1 cup grated Monterey Jack cheese
3/4 lb. fresh asparagus, steamed and diced
1/4 cup red bell pepper, diced
3 eggs
1 1/2 cups whole milk or half-and-half
1 tsp. salt
Pinch black pepper

Preheat oven to 400°. Prepare pie crust according to a favorite recipe, fit into glass pie dish and bake crust 10 minutes. Remove pie shell from oven and cool slightly.

Turn oven down to 350°. Sprinkle grated cheese over crust. Top with diced asparagus and bell pepper. Combine eggs, milk, salt and pepper and pour over asparagus. Bake 1 hour or until custard tests done — when mixture does not adhere to knife when inserted in center. Yield: 6 servings.

▲ ▲ ▲

Rebel souffle

Rebel souffle is a different grits recipe. It has been in my files for more than 25 years and is a favorite for Sunday or holiday brunch. It's especially good for a Big Orange crowd and is different from the usual cheese grits served at parties. The original recipe called for the bacon, but we seldom use it. The recipe can be cut in half.

1 cup quick cooking grits
1 tsp. salt
3 cups boiling water
1/4 cup butter or margarine
1 cup orange juice

1 tsp. shredded orange rind
3 eggs, slightly beaten
12 slices cooked bacon (optional)
Brown sugar

Preheat oven to 350°. Slowly stir grits into boiling salted water. Cook 3 to 5 minutes, stirring constantly. The mixture should be slightly thickened. Remove from heat, add butter or margarine, orange juice and orange rind. Gently stir in the eggs. Pour into buttered 2-quart baking dish. Top with cooked bacon, if desired. Sprinkle brown sugar over the top. Bake about 45 minutes or until mixture does not adhere to knife when inserted in center. Yield: 8 servings.

▲ ▲ ▲

Butterscotch pie

This recipe for butterscotch (or caramel) pie comes from Mrs. Frank Quarles in Jefferson City. She says the recipe took a prize at a Malone, Ky., school in 1922. It is absolutely wonderful and is very, very rich. You do need an iron skillet to caramelize the brown sugar mixture. If you don't have an iron skillet, skip on to the next recipe.

1 (8-inch) baked and cooled pie shell
1 cup brown sugar
3 Tbsp. butter (no substitute)
4 Tbsp. whipping cream (or evaporated milk)
1 cup whole milk (or evaporated light milk)
1 egg yolk
6 Tbsp. all-purpose flour
Meringue topping or whipped topping

Meringue:
3 egg whites
1/4 tsp. cream of tartar
5 Tbsp. sugar

Prepare pie crust according to a favorite recipe, fit into glass pie dish and bake, according to recipe directions. Remove from oven and cool.

Combine brown sugar, butter and cream in iron skillet over very low heat. Using long-handled spoon, cook and stir mixture until it is thick and brown, about 8 to 10 minutes. The browner it gets, the more butterscotch (or caramel) taste it has. To avoid burning, remove from heat and let caramel set a few minutes.

Combine the milk, egg yolk and flour, mixing well. When sugar mixture is caramelized, stir in flour mixture, stirring constantly. Cook until thick. Pour into baked pie crust.

Prepare meringue: In a small, deep bowl, beat egg whites with electric mixer until frothy. Add cream of tartar and beat on high speed until whites are stiff, but not dry, until they stand in peaks that lean over slightly when beater is withdrawn. Very gradually add the sugar, about a tablespoon at a time. Beat until whites are fairly stiff, but still glossy.

Spread on the hot filling, sealing well to the edges of the crust. Bake at 350° for 12 to 15 minutes, until golden brown.

To cut: Dip a sharp knife into hot water after each slice for a perfect serving.

Yield: 6 servings.

▲ ▲ ▲
Louise's fudge cake

The following chocolate fudge cake is a favorite of favorites and has been in my collection for more than 25 years. I prefer it with fudge icing, but a friend likes to make it with caramel icing (see recipe on next page). Take your pick.

3/4 cup butter or margarine
2 1/4 cups sugar
1 1/2 tsp. vanilla
3 eggs
3 (1-oz.) squares unsweetened chocolate
3 cups all-purpose flour
1 1/2 tsp. soda
3/4 tsp. salt
1 1/2 cups ice water

Preheat oven to 350°. Beat together the butter or margarine, sugar and vanilla. Add eggs, one at a time, and beat until mixture is light and fluffy. Melt the chocolate and add to butter mixture. Sift together the flour, soda and salt and add to the batter, alternately with ice water.

Grease and line with wax paper three 8-inch layer cake pans. Divide batter between pans. Bake near middle of preheated oven 30 to 35 minutes or until toothpick inserted near center comes out clean. Do not overbake.

Cool in pans on wire rack 10 minutes. Loosen sides of cake from pan with a thin knife and invert cakes onto wire rack. Finish cooling before frosting.

The cake can be baked in a 9-by-13-inch pan. Bake for 45 minutes.

Fudge frosting:
1/2 cup butter, softened
5 cups sifted confectioners' sugar
1/2 cup cream or milk
Dash salt
3 squares unsweetened chocolate, melted
2 tsp. vanilla

Combine ingredients, adding enough of 1/2 cup cream or milk to make icing of spreading consistency. Beat until smooth with electric mixer.

Caramel icing:
2 cups brown sugar
1 cup cream or 1/2 cup butter plus 1/2 cup milk
3 Tbsp. butter
1 tsp. vanilla
Cream
Chopped nuts (optional)

Stir over low heat the brown sugar and 1 cup cream (or the butter and milk) until the sugar is dissolved. Cover and cook for about 3 minutes or until the steam has washed down any crystals, which may have formed on the sides of the pan. Uncover and cook without stirring to 238° to 240° on candy thermometer. Add the 3 tablespoons butter. Remove the icing from the heat and cool to 110°. Add vanilla and beat the icing until it is thick and creamy. If it becomes too heavy, thin it with a little cream until it is of the right consistency to be spread.

Top with chopped nuts, if desired. Makes about 1 1/2 cups.

▲ ▲ ▲

Just as it takes farmers and grocers and lots of other folks to help get a tasty dish on the dinner table, it has taken the efforts of a number of News-Sentinel staffers to launch this cookbook. I especially thank Editor Harry Moskos for making this project possible; public service director Susan Alexander for organizing and putting the text together; artists Jerry Weintz and Charlie Daniel for the cover artwork and inside sketches, respectively; photographer J. Miles Cary for the back cover photo; retired features staffer Christine Anderson, for carefully checking each recipe to make sure we didn't say tablespoon when we meant to say teaspoon; and columnist Sam Venable, for lending his proofreading assistance, too.

– Louise Durman
April 1992

Appetizers and soups

▲ ▲ ▲

Appetizers and soups

▲ ▲ ▲

Cheese straws

Alberta Brewer, Norris, wife of retired News-Sentinel columnist Carson Brewer, makes the best cheese straws, we were told when we went searching for a recipe. She shares her recipe and adds special instructions.

1 lb. sharp cheese	Salt to taste
1/2 lb. butter or margarine	Red pepper to taste
3 cups flour	Worcestershire sauce to taste

Grate cheese and cream butter. Mix together. Add flour and seasonings. Using pastry press (star plate), make long strips with the batter the entire length of the cookie sheet. Bake at 375° for 8 to 10 minutes. Cut immediately into desired lengths.

Brewer adds: "I have had the best results using Cracker Barrel Extra Sharp cheese and real butter. I also mix dough with my hands and know the dough is the right consistency when it pulls free of the sides of the bowl and the hands easily. A little flour may be added to achieve this, if necessary.

"With real sharp cheese, I use no salt. Usually I find about 1/4 tsp. red pepper and 1/2 tsp. Worcestershire suit our tastes."

▲ ▲ ▲

Mexican cream cheese rollups

Several readers sent recipes for Mexican rollup or tortilla rolls in answer to a request. Carolyn Wilson, Chino Hills, Calif., wrote:
"In case you wonder why I read your paper —my husband is an avid Vols fan and has subscribed to the paper for years from all across the country during 37 years of being transferred by his company."
Here is her version:

1 (8-oz.) pkg. cream cheese, softened

1/3 cup mayonnaise

1 (4.25-oz.) can chopped olives, drained

6 green onions, washed and trimmed, finely chopped, including green tops

Several soft large flour tortillas

Mix cream cheese and mayonnaise until well blended. Stir in olives and onions. Spread a thin layer of cream cheese mixture over tortilla, leaving a half-inch border around the edge with no filling. Roll tortilla up and wrap in plastic wrap.

Continue in same manner until all filling has been used. Refrigerate several hours or until firm. Cut into 1 1/2-inch slices and serve with favorite salsa, if desired, for dipping. Yield: 6 to 8 servings.

▲ ▲ ▲

Fried mozzarella

Jeanne Ennis, Knoxville, contributes a recipe for fried mozzarella. She says it is similar to the appetizer served at T.G.I. Friday's.

1 lb. mozzarella
2 cups fresh, plain bread crumbs
1 Tbsp. oregano
1 Tbsp. basil
1/4 tsp. salt
1/2 tsp. black pepper
2 eggs
1/4 cup milk
Marinara sauce (recipe follows)

Cut the cheese into 1/4-inch thick, finger-sized pieces. In a shallow bowl, toss the bread crumbs with oregano, basil, salt and pepper. In another bowl, beat eggs and milk. Dip cheese into egg-milk mixture, then coat with bread crumbs. Dip again into egg mixture. Dredge a second time in crumbs. Repeat double coatings for each strip of cheese. Set on a platter until ready to fry.

In a heavy frying pan, heat 1 inch of oil until it ripples. Have a few paper towels nearby. Using scissor tongs, place cheese in the oil and quickly fry a few pieces at a time, giving them less than a minute per side. (The oil must be very hot and the frying must be done immediately or the cheese will ooze from inside its coating.) Drain on paper towels. Arrange side by side on a long platter. Spoon a strip of marinara sauce down the middle of platter. Serve hot with extra sauce. Makes about 16 pieces.

Marinara sauce:
2 (15-oz.) cans tomato sauce with tomato bits
1 clove garlic, minced
2 tsp. olive oil
3 Tbsp. chopped parsley
1/3 cup dry white wine
1/2 tsp. basil
1/4 tsp. oregano
1/2 tsp. sugar
Few grinds of pepper

Saute garlic in olive oil. Add remaining ingredients. Simmer 1 1/2 hours or until thick, stirring occasionally. Extra sauce may be stored in a jar in the refrigerator. Reheat when ready to serve.

▲ ▲ ▲

Beer-cheese ball

This tangy cheese ball comes from Becky Swann of Jefferson City.

10 oz. sharp Cracker Barrel cheese
2 (8-oz.) pkgs. cream cheese, softened
1 tsp. garlic powder
1 medium onion, chopped
2 Tbsp. or more Worcestershire sauce
2 Tbsp. beer (or enough to moisten)
Pecans

Grate onion. Put cheese in food processor and grate. Add onion and mix. Add other ingredients (except pecans), beating with electric mixer. Form into ball, top with pecans. Serve with assorted crackers. Cheese ball keeps well in refrigerator or may be frozen several months.

▲ ▲ ▲

Fruit and cheese ball

A different and delicious fruit and cheese ball recipe comes from Johanna Parkins of Morristown.

1 (8-oz.) pkg. cream cheese
1 cup shredded sharp cheddar cheese
1 Tbsp. honey
1 (6-oz.) pkg. mixed dry fruit tidbits
Chopped pecans

Combine cheeses and honey. Mix in fruit and shape into ball. Roll in chopped pecans.

▲ ▲ ▲

Holiday cheese ball

Here is a cheese ball recipe from Ailene Blair of Knoxville.

2 oz. cheddar cheese, cubed
1 small wedge onion
3 oz. blue cheese
6 oz. cream cheese
2 Tbsp. milk
1/2 tsp. Worcestershire sauce
1/2 cup pecans
4 sprigs fresh parsley

Place cheddar cheese and onion in food processor and pulse 3 to 4 times. Add blue cheese, cream cheese, milk and Worcestershire. Blend well. Empty onto plastic wrap and shape in ball or log. Refrigerate overnight.

One hour before serving, place pecans and parsley in food processor and chop fine. Roll ball or log in mixture. Place on serving tray with crackers. Yield: 1 1/2 cups.

If preparing in a blender: Put milk in blender container first; add blue cheese. Blend and while it is processing, add cheddar cheese, onion, Worcestershire sauce and cream cheese. Blend until smooth and follow above directions, chopping pecans and parsley in the blender.

▲ ▲ ▲

Feta cheese spread

1 (8-oz.) pkg. cream cheese, softened
1 (8-oz.) pkg. feta cheese
1/4 cup pine nuts (optional)
1/4 cup black olives
1/4 cup chopped parsley
3 Tbsp. mayonnaise
1 clove garlic
2 Tbsp. coarsely chopped onion
1 Tbsp. lemon juice
Coarsely ground black pepper to taste

Blend ingredients in food processor until mixture makes a smooth spread. If blended by hand, chop garlic finely first. Also chopped nuts and olives. Store in a tightly closed container. Refrigerate overnight to let flavors blend. Serve with crackers.

▲ ▲ ▲

Olive nut spread

Polly Harrison, Crossville, shares a recipe for a spread made with cream cheese and olives. It's not necessary to add salt, Harrison cautions.

1 (8-oz.) pkg. cream cheese, softened
1/2 cup mayonnaise
3/4 cup chopped pecans or walnuts
1 cup chopped green or ripe olives
1 Tbsp. Dijon mustard
2/3 cup finely chopped celery
2 Tbsp. finely chopped green pepper
2 Tbsp. onion juice or minced onion

Combine all ingredients, mixing well. Serve with chips, crackers or vegetables.

▲ ▲ ▲

Zippy beef olive spread

2 1/2 tsp. instant minced onion
1/4 to 1/2 cup dry white wine
1 (8-oz.) pkg. cream cheese
2 Tbsp. mayonnaise
1 (3-oz.) pkg. smoked sliced (dried) beef
1/2 cup chopped pimento-stuffed olives

Soften minced onion in wine. Blend together cream cheese and mayonnaise. Add wine-onion mixture. Snip finely the sliced beef and add to mixture; add olives. Serve at room temperature with crackers.

▲ ▲ ▲

Artichoke dip

1 (12-oz.) can artichoke hearts, drained and halved
1/4 cup sour cream
1/2 cup mayonnaise
1/2 cup Parmesan cheese

Place artichoke hearts in a blender or food processor and blend until smooth. Add remaining ingredients and process again. Remove, place in baking dish and bake in 350° oven for 20 minutes or heat in the microwave for 3 minutes. Serve with a variety of crackers and sliced raw vegetables.

▲ ▲ ▲

Beef dip

Tonya Dukes of Knoxville shares a recipe for beef dip.

1 (8-oz.) pkg. cream cheese
1/2 cup sour cream
2 Tbsp. instant minced onions
1/4 cup chopped walnuts
2 Tbsp. milk
1 small jar dried beef, finely chopped
1/2 tsp. pepper
3 shakes Worcestershire sauce

Mix all ingredients over low heat until blended. Serve from fondue pot.

▲ ▲ ▲

Chili cheese dip

From Ailene Blair of Knoxville comes a spicy dip for the fondue pot.

1 (15-oz.) can chili without beans
1 lb. processed American cheese, cut into 1-inch cubes
1 (4-oz.) can diced green chilies
Corn chips

Put all ingredients except corn chips into fondue pot over medium heat. Stir occasionally until cheese has melted. Reduce heat to low. Dip corn chips into mixture. Yield: 3 cups.

▲ ▲ ▲

Dilly rye dip

2/3 cup sour cream
2/3 cup mayonnaise
1 tsp. dill weed
1 tsp. Beau Monde seasoning (a blend)
1 Tbsp. dried minced onion
1 Tbsp. parsley flakes
1 large round loaf of unsliced rye bread

Combine all ingredients except bread and refrigerate for 24 hours. When ready to serve, scoop out center of unsliced rye bread to use as a "bowl." Put dip into bread bowl. Break the scooped-out bread into small pieces for dipping. The dip is also good with vegetables and/or chips.

▲ ▲ ▲

Mexican dip

Johanna Parkins of Morristown serves this layered dip with tortilla chips.

1 (8-oz.) pkg. cream cheese, softened
1 cup medium salsa (or mild or hot, depending on taste)
1 can chili without beans
1 (8-oz.) pkg. hot pepper cheese, grated

Spread cream cheese on bottom of baking dish. Layer remaining ingredients in order given. Bake at 350° for 20 to 30 minutes until bubbly.

▲ ▲ ▲

Shrimp dip

This delicious shrimp dip from Donna Colburn of The News-Sentinel staff resembles a pizza because of its layers.

1 1/2 to 2 (8-oz.) pkgs. soft cream cheese
6 (4-oz.) jars shrimp cocktail
6 green onions, chopped, including tops
2 cups pizza cheese (mozzarella, Swiss, etc.)

Spread cream cheese on a platter (approx. 12" diameter). Sprinkle half of pizza cheese on top. Spread all shrimp cocktail sauce over top evenly. Sprinkle with chopped onions and add remaining cheese. Chill and serve with crackers. May be prepared a day ahead. Serves 16 to 18.

▲ ▲ ▲

Snowcrab dip

*Richard Helms of The News-Sentinel marketing staff worked out this recipe.
He shreds the crab meat by hand — a food processor chops it too finely.*

2 to 2 1/2 pounds imitation or real crab meat
1 to 1 1/2 cups mayonnaise
16 oz. sour cream
16 oz. cream cheese, softened

Drain and shred crab meat by hand. Use electric hand mixer to mix all ingredients. Cover and chill overnight. Serve with crackers or vegetables.

▲ ▲ ▲

Spicy black-eyed pea dip

Vicki Hollingsworth Caldwell of Knoxville offers this recipe.

2 cans black-eyed peas
5 canned jalapeno peppers
1 Tbsp. jalapeno juice from can
1 (4-oz.) can green chilies
1/2 medium onion, chopped
1 clove garlic or garlic powder

1/2 lb. sharp cheddar cheese
1 to 1 1/2 sticks melted butter

Combine first six ingredients in blender or food processor. Melt cheese and butter together. Combine with pea mixture. Serve warm with large corn chips.

▲ ▲ ▲

Vegetable dip

Nancy Baker of Dandridge serves this dill-flavored dip with fresh vegetables.

1 pkg. original Hidden Valley Ranch salad dressing mix
1 pint sour cream
1 pint mayonnaise
3 Tbsp. chopped fresh parsley
2 Tbsp. dried dill weed
1 Tbsp. seasoned salt
2 Tbsp. grated onion

Combine ingredients and chill overnight. Serve with raw vegetables.

▲ ▲ ▲

Honey picante chicken wings

16-18 medium-size chicken wings (about 3 lbs.)
3/4 cup picante sauce
1/4 cup honey
1 1/2 Tbsp. Dijon-style mustard

Cut off tip of wings at first joint of each wing. Cut the remaining wing into two parts at the joint. Combine picante sauce, honey and mustard in a small saucepan; bring to a boil. Reduce heat and simmer 12 to 14 minutes or until thickened, stirring occasionally.

Place chicken in foil-lined baking pan. Brush with half of picante sauce mixture. Bake at 350° for 20 minutes. Turn and brush with half of remaining sauce. Bake 10 to 15 minutes, basting occasionally with remaining sauce. Serve warm or at room temperature with additional picante sauce, if desired.

▲ ▲ ▲

Meatballs in cranberry and tomato sauce

Bernice Stevens, Gatlinburg, sends a recipe for meatballs that Mrs. I. J. Breman
brought to a covered dish luncheon in Oak Ridge some 25 years ago.

1 1/2 lbs. ground chuck
1 can whole cranberry sauce
1 (10 3/4-oz.) can tomato puree

Form meatballs from ground chuck and brown. Drain, then add cranberry sauce and tomato puree. Simmer for 2 1/2 hours in sauce. Serve from a chafing dish as an appetizer or over cooked rice or pasta.

▲ ▲ ▲

Sauerkraut balls

*The many versions we received for making sauerkraut balls surprised us.
Usually they are served as appetizers, but one reader says they are good for a
winter meal. Serve with hot potato soup and fruit for dessert. Tamra Brown,
Knoxville, sent this recipe.*

2 lbs. sauerkraut

1/2 lb. each ham, corned beef and lean pork

1/3 cup finely chopped onion

3 Tbsp. butter or margarine

2 cups flour

1 tsp. dry mustard

1/2 tsp. salt

1 3/4 cups milk

1 cup bread crumbs

1/2 cup flour

3/4 cup milk

Simmer sauerkraut in saucepan for 1/2 hour (longer for milder taste).
Drain. Grind ham, corned beef and pork. Saute the meats and onion in
butter in skillet until pork is no longer pink. Add flour, dry mustard, salt, and
1 3/4 cups milk. Simmer until mixture is thickened, stirring constantly.

Add sauerkraut. Regrind the entire mixture. Refrigerate about an hour
or until mixture is cool and easy to work with. Mold into balls.

Mix together the 1/2 cup flour and 3/4 cup milk. Dip the balls into the
flour-milk mixture and roll in bread crumbs. Heat oil to about 365° and
deep fry balls until they are golden brown. Drain on paper towels and
serve.

▲ ▲ ▲

Asparagus rolls

Bill Orr of Jefferson City makes these wonderful treats.

1 (about 2-lb.) loaf white bread
2 cans asparagus spears (not pieces)
1 (8-oz.) pkg. cream cheese
1 heaping Tbsp. blue cheese
1 stick butter or margarine, melted

Flatten bread with rolling pin and trim off crusts. Drain asparagus spears on paper towel. Combine cream cheese and blue cheese, beating until smooth. Spread cheese on bread slices in thin layer. Then place 1 stalk asparagus at one end of bread slice and roll up the bread.

Melt butter or margarine in small skillet and turn the asparagus roll in the melted butter, coating both sides well. Place a piece of foil on a cookie or baking sheet. Spray foil with Pam. Place asparagus rolls on the foil, and if desired, freeze at this point. Thaw about half way and bake at 350° for 15 to 20 minutes, until lightly brown. Turn rolls over and brown on other side.When baking is finished, cut each roll into thirds.

The rolls may be sprinkled with Parmesan cheese after they are baked.

▲ ▲ ▲

Layered guacamole

Johanna Parkins of Morristown sends a recipe for a delicous dip to serve with tortilla chips. Ingredients fill a large 11-by-15-inch dish; it serves a crowd.

2 large avocados, peeled
1 Tbsp. lemon juice
1/8 tsp. garlic salt
1/4 tsp. garlic powder
2 Tbsp. finely minced onion
2 Tbsp. mayonnaise
1 (1-lb.) can refried beans
1 cup sour cream
2 jars hot picante sauce, drained in a sieve
1 large can pitted black olives, drained and chopped
1 1/2 cups shredded cheddar cheese
1 cup chopped tomato

Combine with mixer until smooth the avocados, lemon juice, garlic salt, garlic powder, onion and mayonnaise. In 11-by-15-inch dish layer in order: refried beans, avocado mixture, sour cream, picante sauce, olives, cheddar cheese and tomato. Chill until ready to serve.

▲ ▲ ▲

Marinated brussels sprouts

1 pkg. frozen brussels sprouts
1 small bottle Seven Seas Viva Italian salad dressing
1 tsp. dill weed (or more to taste)
1 Tbsp. finely minced onion

Cook brussels sprouts until almost done, but still crunchy. Mix all other ingredients. Pour over sprouts and marinate overnight in the refrigerator in a deep bowl so dressing completely covers the sprouts. Serve chilled.

▲ ▲ ▲

Sweet potato spiders

This recipe is for an appetizer that was served at the old L &N Restaurant in Knoxville.

1 Tbsp. oil
1 egg
7 Tbsp. all-purpose flour
4 Tbsp. water
1/4 tsp. salt
1/2 tsp. baking powder
2 medium sweet potatoes
Oil for frying
Confectioners' sugar (optional)

For coating, combine oil, egg, flour, water, salt and baking powder. Shred potatoes. Using your fingers, take a dab of potatoes and dip in coating mixture. Drop into about 3 inches of heated oil in deep saucepan or "Fry Daddy" (a skillet doesn't work well) and fry until golden brown. It may be necessary to turn them. Remove from oil and roll in sugar, if desired.

▲ ▲ ▲

Asparagus soup

For the lunch served at the Talahi Park plant sale during the Dogwood Arts Festival, Melissa Gill, Knoxville, has made this soup.

1 stick butter
1 small onion, grated
2 chicken bouillon cubes dissolved in 2 cups boiling water
2 stalks celery, chopped
1 medium to large potato, chopped
Salt and pepper to taste
1 pint half-and-half (milk and cream)
1 lb. fresh asparagus, cut into 1-inch pieces, reserving the tips

Melt butter in saucepan. Saute onions; add chicken bouillon, celery, potatoes, salt and pepper; cook until potatoes are tender. Add asparagus and half-and-half; simmer 10 to 15 minutes. Process in food processor or blender until nearly smooth; pour into saucepan and keep mixture warm.

Set aside enough asparagus tips, one per serving, for garnish. Chop rest of the reserved tips finely and saute in butter. When serving, place spoonful of sauteed asparagus tips with liquid into bottom of soup bowl. Add soup. Garnish with raw asparagus tip. Yield: 8 to 10 servings.

▲ ▲ ▲

* Bean soup

Ginger Branch, West Parkway, says her family likes this on a cold winter day.

1 cup EACH pinto, navy, large lima and great northern beans
Ham bone and ham hock
1 cup chopped celery
1 cup chopped onion
1 cup chopped carrots
1 large can tomatoes
1 green pepper, chopped
Parsley
1 minced garlic clove
1 tsp. oregano
1 tsp. basil
Salt, pepper

Soak beans overnight in cold water to cover. Drain. Simmer ham bone and hock in water to cover for 30 minutes. Add beans, celery, onion, carrots, tomatoes, green pepper, parsley, garlic and spices. Cook half a day, adding more water or chicken broth as needed. Freezes well.

▲ ▲ ▲

Little kettle bean soup

Bill and Joyce Maples, Knoxville, think this is the best bean soup. They say it is similar to the soup at Peroulas' Quality Food at Market Square.

1 lb. dried navy beans
2 1/2 qts. water
3/4 cup celery, diced
3/4 cup carrots, diced
1 medium onion, chopped
1 meaty ham bone or hock
1/2 cup hot barbecue sauce
1/4 lb. bacon ends and pieces
 1 Tbsp. salt (or to taste)
1/4 tsp. pepper
1/8 tsp. garlic powder

Soak beans overnight in large amount of water. Next morning drain and add the 2 1/2 quarts water. Add remaining ingredients. Bring to a boil, turn down heat and cover. Simmer 4 hours or until beans reach desired tenderness. Add additional water if necessary as it simmers.

▲ ▲ ▲

Beer cheese soup

1/4 cup margarine
1/2 cup chopped onion
1/2 cup shredded carrot
1/4 cup all-purpose flour
Dash of salt and pepper
2 1/2 cups milk
1 (16-oz.) jar Cheez Whiz
1/2 cup beer

Melt margarine in saucepan. Add chopped onion and shredded carrot. Cook until tender. Blend in flour, salt and pepper. Add milk, stirring constantly until thickened. Add Cheez Whiz. Stir to melt. Blend in beer. Heat and serve. Yield: 4 servings.

▲ ▲ ▲

Broccoli cheese soup

Nita Noe of Knoxville provides this recipe.

2 (10-oz.) pkgs. frozen chopped broccoli
3 cans chicken broth
1/2 stick margarine
1 onion, chopped
2 cups milk
1/2 cup flour
1 lb. grated Velveeta cheese
Dash of pepper

Simmer broccoli in chicken broth for 15 minutes. Melt margarine in pan. Add onions and saute. Add flour to onion and stir well. Add milk gradually and stir until thick. Stir into broccoli. Add grated cheese and stir until melted. Add pepper. Do not let mixture boil. Yield: 4 servings.

▲ ▲ ▲

Creamy broccoli soup

Carolyn Catlett, Sevierville, sends a recipe for creamy broccoli soup.

2 cups chopped fresh broccoli
1 cup boiling water
1/4 cup butter
2/3 cup chopped onion
2 Tbsp. flour
2 cups chicken broth
2 cups half-and-half (milk and cream)
1/2 tsp. Worcestershire sauce
3/4 tsp. salt
1 cup grated cheddar cheese

Cook broccoli in 1 cup boiling water. Drain, reserving liquid.
Melt butter. Add onion and cook until soft. Blend in flour. Add chicken broth and cook, stirring constantly, until mixture comes to a boil. Stir in 1 cup liquid drained from broccoli, adding water if necessary to make one cup. Add half-and-half, Worcestershire sauce and salt. Add broccoli. Heat to boiling. Stir in cheese. Yield: 4 to 6 servings.

▲ ▲ ▲

Cabbage soup

A Clinton reader sends us a soup recipe that she says tastes like the soup
Shoney's serves. It calls for a lot of salt and pepper; you may want to adjust.

3/4 lb. ground beef
3/4 cup chopped onions
3/4 cup chopped green peppers
4 oz. tomato paste
2 lbs. cabbage, shredded
1/2 cup Worcestershire sauce
1 gallon water

1 (18 3/4-oz.) can tomatoes
4 beef bouillon cubes
1 Tbsp. salt
1 cup catsup
1 Tbsp. sugar
1 Tbsp. black pepper

Brown meat lightly in large heavy pot. Add remaining ingredients and simmer until done. Soup freezes well.

▲ ▲ ▲

Chicken and ham gumbo

1 medium onion, chopped
1 tsp. margarine
1 qt. chicken broth
2 cups cooked chicken, cut in cubes
1 cup ham, julienne strips or cubes
1/2 cup frozen whole-kernel corn, thawed; or canned, drained
2 cups canned tomatoes and juice
1 clove garlic, minced
1/4 tsp. marjoram
1/4 tsp. thyme
Salt, pepper to taste
1 pkg. frozen okra, cooked and strained
Cooked rice

Stir-fry chopped onion in melted margarine. In stock pot or large kettle, combine all ingredients except okra and cooked rice. Bring to a boil and let simmer. Meanwhile cook frozen okra in salted water. Bring okra to a boil, turn to simmer and let it cook until it clots — about 5 minutes. Strain to get the roping off the okra. Add to ingredients in stock pot. Place scoop of hot cooked rice in large bowls and spoon gumbo over rice. Yield: 8 to 10 servings.

▲ ▲ ▲

Chili con carne

Jane Yancey, former owner with her husband Joe of Cat's Meow Restaurant in the University of Tennessee area, sends a recipe for the chili served at the restaurant before it closed in 1973.

1 lb. ground beef
1 Tbsp. shortening
1/3 cup onion flakes
2 to 3 Tbsp. chili powder
1 tsp. salt
Dash garlic powder
1 (8-oz.) can tomato sauce
1 (16-oz. or 28-oz.) can tomatoes
2 1/2 cups canned pinto beans
2 Tbsp. vinegar

Brown ground beef in shortening. Add other ingredients and simmer 45 minutes. Add water if mixture becomes too thick, especially if the 16-oz. can of tomatoes is used.

▲ ▲ ▲

Super chili

Cynthia McMeans of Knoxville prepared this chili for a Super Bowl television party.

2 (16-oz.) cans tomatoes, undrained
4 cups water
5 lbs. coarsely chopped lean beef
2 large onions, diced
2 green peppers, diced
3 cloves garlic, minced
4 bay leaves, broken
2 tsp. oregano
4 tsp. ground cumin
2 tsp. salt
6 Tbsp. chili powder
Cayenne or black pepper
1 tsp. coriander

Puree tomatoes in a blender. Pour water and tomatoes into a 1 1/2- or 2-gallon kettle and begin cooking over medium heat. Brown beef, onions and green peppers in skillet; add to tomatoes. Add garlic, bay leaves, oregano, cumin, salt, chili powder and pepper. Bring to a boil, reduce heat and simmer 2 to 3 hours. Add water if mixture gets too thick during cooking. Add coriander 30 minutes before chili is served. Yield: 1 gallon.

Note: Beans may be added to the chili if desired. Chili is best made at least one day before serving and refrigerated overnight.

▲ ▲ ▲

Cream of tomato soup

Kay Rodgers of Knoxville offers this recipe.

12 very ripe tomatoes, peeled and cut up
1 cup canned beef bouillon (or 2 bouillon cubes dissolved in 1 cup boiling water)
1 cup sliced celery
1/2 onion, sliced
1/4 cup minced fresh parsley
3 Tbsp. cornstarch
3 Tbsp. butter, melted
2 Tbsp. brown sugar
2 tsp. salt
Fresh black pepper
2 cups 2% milk
1 egg yolk (optional)

Put tomatoes, bouillon, celery, onions, parsley in a large stock pot. Simmer 30 minutes. Puree and strain. Mix butter and cornstarch. Stir into soup. Add sugar, salt and pepper. When ready to serve, add milk and egg yolk to hot soup. Yield: 6 servings.

▲ ▲ ▲

Cucumber soup

Lyn Regas, formerly of Knoxville, who now lives in Satellite Beach, Fla., likes to make this chilled soup.

2 lbs. cottage cheese
2 Tbsp. to 1/4 cup milk
3 to 4 large cucumbers, peeled, seeded and chopped
2 Tbsp. minced onions, chives or spring onions
1 garlic clove, minced
1 tsp. dill weed
1/2 to 1 tsp. vinegar (or to taste)
Seasoned salt (to taste)
White pepper (to taste)
Sliced cucumbers for garnish
Paprika for garnish

Puree half the cucumbers in a blender; coarsely chop the other half. Combine all ingredients and process in food processor to blend. Chill. Garnish with sliced cucumbers and paprika when ready to serve. Yield: 6 servings.

▲ ▲ ▲

Duchess soup

News-Sentinel features editor Linda Felts Fields brought this recipe back from a New Hampshire country inn.

1/2 cup grated carrots
1/2 cup minced celery
1 cup water
1/4 cup minced onion
1/4 cup butter

1/2 cup flour
2 cups milk
2 cups chicken stock
1/2 lb. cheddar cheese, grated
Chopped parsley, for garnish

Simmer carrots and celery in water till tender. Saute onion in butter until soft. Add flour and blend well. Add milk and chicken stock and cook until thickened. Add cheese and cooked carrots and celery with their cooking water. Top with chopped parsley. Yield: 4 servings.

▲ ▲ ▲

Hamburger-veggie soup

A nourishing soup made with ground beef comes from Sue Cox of Knoxville. It may be varied easily — barley may replace the rice, and other vegetables, such as corn, green beans and kidney beans, are also good in it.

1 to 2 lbs. ground beef
1 large onion, diced
4 sliced carrots
4 stalks celery, cut in 1/2-inch pieces
4 diced potatoes
1/2 small cabbage, sliced (optional)
1 (No. 2 1/2) can tomatoes (3 1/2 cups)
1/4 cup rice, macaroni or broken spaghetti
1 small bay leaf
1/2 tsp. thyme
1/2 tsp. basil
1/4 tsp. dill weed
4 tsp. salt
1/2 tsp. pepper
1 quart water

Brown ground meat and onion in large kettle. Drain off fat. Add carrots, celery, tomatoes and water. Bring to a boil. Add rice. Simmer about 30 minutes. Add potatoes, herbs, spices and cook until done, about 30 minutes. Add cabbage last (about 5 minutes before serving.)
  If soup is too thick, thin with tomato juice or water.

▲ ▲ ▲

Portuguese soup

Joe Ann Phillips of Knoxville has prepared this soup for Ivan Racheff Park and Gardens' craft and plant sale. This is a soup that can be done in a slow cooker.

1 1/2 lbs. Polish sausage, sliced into coin shapes
6 cups water
2 (16-oz.) cans red kidney beans
1/2 dozen carrots, chopped
1 small head cabbage, chopped
1 onion, chopped
4 medium potatoes, peeled and diced
1/2 green pepper, diced
2 (8-oz.) cans tomato sauce
Garlic buds, to taste (see note below)
Salt, pepper to taste

Simmer sausage in 3 cups water for at least 30 minutes. Add other ingredients and simmer at least an hour. Yield: 12 servings.

Note: Phillips crushes the garlic buds and puts them in a cheesecloth bag so she can remove before serving.

▲ ▲ ▲

Potato-bacon chowder

If you use red-skinned potatoes, leave the skins on, says Kayla Carruth, director for health education at the University of Tennessee Medical Center.

8 strips bacon, cut up
1 cup chopped onion
2 cups (or more) potatoes, cubed
1 cup water
1/2 tsp. salt
Dash pepper
1 can cream of chicken soup
1 cup sour cream
1 3/4 cups milk
2 Tbsp. chopped parsley

Cook bacon until crisp in 3-quart saucepan. Add onion, saute 3 minutes. Pour off drippings. Add potatoes, water, salt and pepper. Bring to a boil. Cover, simmer 10 to 15 minutes or until potatoes are tender.

Gradually stir in chicken soup, sour cream, milk and parsley. Bring to serving temperature over low heat, stirring occasionally. Do not boil.

▲ ▲ ▲

Potato soup

Wanda Holt, Manchester, sends a soup recipe that she thinks is like Shoney's.

2 cups diced potatoes
3/4 cup minced onion
2 1/2 tsp. salt
Black or white pepper, to taste
1/2 cup chopped celery
2 1/2 cups boiling water
4 Tbsp. margarine
4 Tbsp. flour
2 cups milk

Combine potatoes, onion, salt, pepper, celery and boiling water in saucepan and cook until tender. Heat butter and flour in skillet until butter melts and flour is dissolved. Add milk and cook until the mixture begins to thicken. Pour over the potato mixture and continue to cook and stir 2 or 3 minutes more. Yield: 2 or 3 servings.

▲ ▲ ▲

Potato-leek soup

Mary Chester of Norris offers this advice about using leeks: It is important to clean them well because they are often full of sand or dirt. Chester places them, root side up, in a jar of water and shakes so water penetrates the stalks. Drain in a colander.

2 medium potatoes
1 small bunch leeks or 2 large leeks
2 qts. chicken broth
1 cup chicken, cooked and chopped
1/2 stick butter or margarine
Salt, pepper to taste

Peel and cube or slice potatoes. Slice leeks in 1/4-inch rounds. Combine all ingredients in large pot and cook over medium heat until potatoes are done. Serve with cornbread. Yield: 6 to 8 servings.

▲ ▲ ▲

Potato soup with ham

Mrs. William Terry, Knoxville, says this soup is a favorite with her husband and their three daughters. The soup is wonderful with a skillet of cornbread, Terry says. She keeps leftover Honey Baked Ham in the freezer to use in her soup.

10 to 12 large potatoes, cut in large diced or cubed pieces (8 cups)
1 cup chopped onion
1 qt. boiling water
1 chicken bouillon cube
3/4 tsp. salt
1 qt. low-fat milk
1 can cream of chicken soup (undiluted)
1 cup plain non-fat yogurt
2 Tbsp. fresh parsley, chopped
1 1/2 cups bite-size pieces of ham

Cook potatoes, onions, salt and chicken bouillon cube in boiling water until potatoes are tender, about 15 minutes. Add remaining ingredients. Bring to serving temperature over low heat, stirring occasionally. Do not boil. Yield: 3 to 4 quarts of soup.

▲ ▲ ▲

Sea Island gumbo

Gumbo is a favorite dish in our household, especially in summer when okra is fresh. This is a recipe we have used for years.

3 cups sliced okra
   (or 1 1/2 pkgs frozen)
1/2 cup melted butter or margarine
1 cup chopped green onions w/ tops
3 cloves garlic, finely chopped
1/2 tsp. pepper
1 tsp. salt (or to taste)

1 cup hot water
1 cup tomato sauce
1 1/2 cups canned tomatoes
2 whole bay leaves
1/2 tsp. Tabasco
1 1/2 lbs. fresh shrimp, cooked
4 cups cooked rice

Cook okra in butter until tender, stirring constantly. Add onion, garlic, salt and pepper. Cook about 5 minutes. Add water, tomato sauce, tomatoes and bay leaves. Add Tabasco and cooked shrimp. Cook again until mixture is very hot, about 5 minutes. Place 1/2 cup cooked rice in bottom of each soup bowl and ladle gumbo over the rice. Yield: 8 servings.

▲ ▲ ▲

Vegetable soup

Lou Brooke of Knoxville shares her mother's vegetable soup recipe.

2 lbs. stew beef
1 soup bone or meat with a bone
4 qts. water
3 beef bouillon cubes or 3 tsp. bouillon beads
2 Tbsp. salt
1/4 tsp. pepper
3 large onions, chopped
1 celery stalk, diced
6 large carrots, sliced thin
1/2 bunch fresh parsley or 3 Tbsp. dried parsley
1/3 head cabbage
3 (1 lb.) cans tomatoes, including juice
2 small cans whole kernel corn
1/2 cup Minute Rice

Bring to a boil the beef, soup bone, water, bouillon, salt and pepper. Skim residue off the top. Add onions, celery, carrots, parsley and cabbage and bring to a boil again. Simmer 30 minutes. Add remaining ingredients and bring to boiling again. Simmer 3 hours. Remove bone. Refrigerate or freeze soup. Skim off fat before reheating.

Salads, dressings and sauces

▲ ▲ ▲

Salads, dressings and sauces

▲ ▲ ▲
Corn bread salad

One of the most popular recipes that's appeared in Recipes & Requests is for corn bread salad. When Elsie Caton of Seymour gave us the recipe, she warned: "If you take the salad to a group get-together, you had better double it." The recipe first came from TVA employee Joe Greene. Other vegetables, such as fresh mushrooms, may be added. The salad may be made ahead and refrigerated.

1 (8 1/2-oz.) pkg. corn muffin mix
1 lb. mild sausage (or bacon or Polish sausage)
1/3 cup sweet bread-and-butter pickles
2 tomatoes
1/2 onion
1/2 green pepper
1/2 cup light or regular mayonnaise
2 Tbsp. pickle juice

Bake corn bread according to directions on package. (Or make a small skilletful of your favorite corn bread.) Cool and crumble the corn bread.

Meanwhile, cook sausage, crumbling it as it cooks. Drain off grease by adding water to sausage, then pouring off water. Drain on paper towels.

Chop pickles, tomatoes, onion and pepper. Add mayonnaise and pickle juice. Stir in sausage and all but 1/2 cup crumbled corn bread. Mix well. Use reserved corn bread to decorate the top. Also garnish with green pepper strips, if desired. Yield: About 6 servings.

▲ ▲ ▲
Taco salad

1 (10-oz.) pkg. corn chips
1 lb. ground beef
1 pkg. dry taco seasoning mix
1 head lettuce, chunky-sliced
1 green pepper, sliced
1 small onion, shredded or sliced
6 oz. cheddar cheese, shredded or cubed
1 tomato, diced
Sour cream

Place 4 cups corn chips in 4-quart bowl or 9-by-13-inch pan. Brown beef in skillet, add taco mix, following directions on package. Set aside. Cut or break up lettuce and put back in refrigerator to crisp. Layer lettuce, pepper and onion on corn chips. Layer cheese, ground beef and tomato on top of onion. Place one cup of corn chips on top. Serve immediately with remaining chips and sour cream. Yield: 6-8 servings.

▲ ▲ ▲

Polynesian chicken salad

Karen Sproles, owner of Knoxville's Lunchbox Restaurant, shares a favorite recipe. Darlene Kerley, News-Sentinel payroll supervisor, worked out proportions.

4 chicken breasts, cooked, deboned and cut up
1 bunch white seedless grapes (about 1 cup)
1 (15 1/4-oz.) can pineapple tidbits, drained
1 carrot, shredded
4 stalks celery, chopped
1 cup mayonnaise
1 cup sour cream
1 Tbsp. lemon juice
1 1/2 to 2 Tbsp. curry powder
1 tsp. salt

Combine chicken, grapes, pineapple, carrot and celery. Mix together mayonnaise, sour cream, lemon juice, curry powder and salt. Gently mix in chicken mixture. Yield: 4 servings.

▲ ▲ ▲

Hot chicken salad

3 cups diced cooked chicken breast
2 cups diced celery
3 Tbsp. minced onion
3 Tbsp. lemon juice
Small jar pimentos, chopped and drained
1 can water chestnuts, drained
3/4 cup mayonnaise
1 can cream of chicken soup
1/2 tsp. salt
1/2 tsp. pepper
Sharp cheese, grated
Crushed potato chips

Mix all ingredients together except grated cheese and potato chips. Place in 9-by-13-inch baking dish. Top with cheese and potato chips. Bake at 325° until heated through, 30 to 45 minutes. Do not freeze. Yield: 6 to 8 servings.

▲ ▲ ▲
Chicken fillet salad

From Betty Finley, Rutledge.

2 whole chicken breasts
4 cups torn lettuce (Boston, red leaf, leaf or a combination)
Creamy raspberry dressing (see recipe in dressings section)
Fresh raspberries for garnish (when available)

Skin and debone chicken breasts. Cut chicken into strips and saute in margarine, just until done. Salt and pepper to taste. Place hot strips on lettuce and serve with raspberry dressing. Garnish with fresh berries. Yield: 2 to 4 servings.

▲ ▲ ▲
Shrimp salad

1 lb. fresh shrimp, shelled and deveined
3/4 cup chopped celery
1/2 cup chopped pecans
1/4 cup chopped stuffed olives or seedless green grapes
1/4 cup French dressing
1/2 cup mayonnaise

Bring 2 quarts water to a boil; drop in shelled shrimp; reduce heat. Cover and simmer 2 to 3 minutes, depending on size of shrimp. Drain shrimp; rinse thoroughly under cold running water.

Cool shrimp. Reserve several to decorate top of salad. Cut remaining into pieces. Combine with celery, pecans and olives or grapes. Chill.

When ready to serve, combine French dressing and mayonnaise. Stir gently into shrimp mixture. Serve on lettuce leaves. Yield: 3 or 4 servings.

▲ ▲ ▲
Shrimp and crab salad

1 lb. fresh shrimp, shelled and deveined
1 (6 1/2-oz.) can crabmeat
1 (8 1/2-oz.) can crushed pineapple, drained
Mayonnaise

Drop shelled shrimp into 2 quarts of boiling water. Reduce heat, cover and simmer 2 to 3 minutes. Drain and rinse shrimp thoroughly under cold running water and set aside to cool.

Drain and flake crabmeat. Drain pineapple (reserve juice to use another time.) Cut up shrimp, reserving a few to use as garnish. Combine shrimp with crabmeat and pineapple. Combine with enough mayonnaise to moisten. Toss lightly. Chill. Yield: 4 servings.

▲ ▲ ▲

Strawberry-asparagus salad

From Betty Finley, Rutledge.

1/4 cup raspberry vinegar	1 lb. fresh asparagus spears
2 Tbsp. oil	2 cups fresh strawberries, sliced
2 Tbsp. honey	Fresh spinach leaves

In jar with tight-fitting lid, combine vinegar, oil and honey. Shake well. Place asparagus spears in skillet with water just covering. Bring quickly to a boil; pour off water immediately. Quick-chill the asparagus in ice water. Drain. Arrange asparagus and berries on fresh spinach with the dressing. Yield: 4 servings.

▲ ▲ ▲

Green bean salad

1 can whole green beans	1/2 cup oil
1 medium onion, sliced into rings	1/2 cup vinegar
1/2 cup sugar	

Drain beans. Slice onion and mix with beans. In a saucepan combine sugar, oil and vinegar. Bring to a boil and pour over beans. Marinate overnight or at least 12 hours. Reheat when ready to serve and serve hot. Yield: 2 to 4 servings.

▲ ▲ ▲

Broccoli salad

This version of broccoli salad comes from News-Sentinel staff writer Ina Hughs.

1/2 cup mayonnaise

1/4 cup sugar

3 Tbsp. vinegar

1 large bunch broccoli, washed; remove stems and leaves and cut into tiny florets

8-10 strips bacon, cooked and crumbled

1/2 cup minced spring onions

1/2 cup chopped pecans

1/2 cup golden raisins

Combine mayonnaise, sugar and vinegar in small bowl. Toss remaining ingredients in a serving bowl. Stir in dressing. Serve chilled. Yield: 8 servings.

Note: Vary salad by using half cauliflower, half broccoli. Add pimento and/or cherry tomatoes.

▲ ▲ ▲

Broccoli salad

From Ailene Blair of Knoxville comes this broccoli salad recipe. She says it disappears quickly.

1 1/2 lbs. fresh broccoli
1/2 cup stuffed green olives, sliced
1 small onion, chopped
4 hard-cooked eggs, shredded
Mayonnaise

Wash and drain fresh broccoli. Cut into florets and small slices; don't use tough part of stalks. Combine broccoli, olives, onions and eggs. Stir in enough mayonnaise to make salad stick together. Yield: 6 to 8 servings.

▲ ▲ ▲

* Marinated vegetables

1 bunch broccoli florets
1 head cauliflower, separated into bite-size florets
8 to 10 oz. fresh mushrooms, sliced
1 green pepper, cut in strips
1 large onion (Vidalia preferred), sliced and separated into rings
1 large can pitted black olives, well drained
1 cup salad oil (corn or canola)
6 Tbsp. lemon juice
10 Tbsp. wine vinegar
4 tsp. salt
4 tsp. pepper
1 tsp. sugar

Place vegetables in large container with tight fitting lid. Combine remaining ingredients and pour over vegetables. Mix well, chill overnight. Yield: 10 to 12 servings.

▲ ▲ ▲
* Cauliflower salad

1 head cauliflower, separated into florets
1 small can sliced dark ripe olives, drained
2/3 cup green pepper slices
1/2 to 1 onion, sliced
1/2 cup pimento (optional)
1/2 to 1 cup fresh mushrooms, sliced (optional)
1/2 cup salad oil
3 Tbsp. lemon juice
5 Tbsp. wine vinegar
2 tsp. salt
2 tsp. pepper
1/2 tsp. sugar

Make dressing by combining salad oil, lemon juice, wine vinegar, salt, pepper (the large amount of pepper is correct), and sugar. Mix well. Pour dressing over vegetables and chill overnight. Yield: 8 to 10 servings.

▲ ▲ ▲
Coleslaw

Frank J. Kotsianas, who owned Kotsi's in Franklin Square and the Brass Rail in downtown Knoxville, answers a request for coleslaw that he originated for the Brass Rail in 1958.

1 head green cabbage, thinly shredded and chopped
1 green pepper, thinly chopped
2 Tbsp. chopped fresh parsley
1 Tbsp. sugar
1/4 tsp. crushed red pepper
1/2 tsp. salt
3 Tbsp. red wine vinegar
2 Tbsp. olive oil

Toss and mix all ingredients until well blended. Serve chilled. Yield: 6 to 8 servings.

▲ ▲ ▲

Freezer slaw

1 head cabbage	1 cup vinegar
1 carrot	1/4 cup water
1 green pepper	1 1/2 cups sugar
1 Tbsp. salt	1 1/2 tsp. mustard seed
	1/2 tsp. celery seed

Shred cabbage, carrot and green pepper and combine. Add salt. Let stand 1 hour and then drain. Combine in saucepan vinegar, water, sugar, mustard seed and celery seed and boil 1 minute. Remove from heat and let cool. Pour over cabbage mixture and freeze in airtight container. Let thaw and serve chilled. Yield: 6 servings.

▲ ▲ ▲

Confederate slaw

Helen Cunningham, Alcoa, contributes a cooked slaw recipe.

1 medium head cabbage	2/3 cup sugar
2 cups salted water	1/2 cup vinegar
Pepper or paprika	2 Tbsp. butter
	2 eggs, beaten

Using sharp knife, shave cabbage very fine to make 3 or 4 cups. Cook in salted water until tender. Drain and put cabbage into a bowl. For dressing, bring to a boil the sugar, vinegar and butter. Add a small amount to well-beaten eggs, then stir eggs into vinegar mixture. Cook one minute, stirring constantly. Pour over cooked cabbage; sprinkle with pepper or paprika. Serve warm or cold. Yield: 6 servings.

▲ ▲ ▲

Refrigerator slaw

Susan Smith, Knoxville, took a 24-hour slaw to a picnic. It drew rave reviews.

1/2 medium head green cabbage	2/3 cup salad oil
1/2 medium head red cabbage	1 Tbsp. celery seed
1 onion, sliced	1 Tbsp. salt
3/4 cup sugar	1 Tbsp. prepared mustard
1 cup vinegar	1/3 cup sugar

Shred cabbage. Combine with onion and 3/4 cup sugar and mix well. Combine remaining ingredients and heat to boiling. Pour over cabbage mixture and mix well. Cover and refrigerate overnight. Will keep a week. Yield: 8 to 10 servings.

▲ ▲ ▲
Cucumber and onion relish

Carolyn Broady, Pigeon Forge, sends a recipe that is a "close facsimile" to the cucumber and onion relish served at Gatlinburg's Pancake Pantry.

1/2 cup sour cream	**1/2 tsp. salt**
1 Tbsp. sugar	**2 medium cucumbers, sliced thin**
1 Tbsp. vinegar	**2 small onions, sliced thin**

Combine sour cream, sugar, vinegar and salt. Add cucumbers and onions, tossing gently. Cover and chill 24 hours, stirring occasionally. Yield: 4 servings.

▲ ▲ ▲
Sweet and sour cucumbers

A version using whipping cream comes from Nancy Thomas, Morristown.

12 medium cucumbers	**2 cups sugar**
2 Tbsp. salt	**1/2 tsp. pepper**
1 medium onion	**1 pint vinegar**
	1 pint whipping cream

Wash, peel and slice cucumbers. Place in earthenware jar. Add salt and sliced onion. Cover jar with cheesecloth, plate and weight. Let stand 6 hours. Drain off water. Add sugar and mix until dissolved. Add pepper and vinegar. Stir in cream. Refrigerate until cold and crisp.

▲ ▲ ▲
Kraut salad

Mrs. W.K. (Billie) McGlothin of Knoxville offers a sauerkraut salad recipe she served when she had guests visiting during the World's Fair.

1 (No. 2) can sauerkraut, drained
1/2 cup chopped green peppers
1/2 cup chopped red sweet peppers
1 cup sugar

Combine ingredients. Store in refrigerator. Yield: 2 to 4 servings.

▲ ▲ ▲

Mandarin orange-almond salad

Nancy Baker, Dandridge, tried recipe after recipe until she had a mandarin orange-romaine lettuce salad identical to the one she first tasted at Atlanta's Magic Pan. It must be tossed at the last minute because the lettuce wilts quickly.

1/2 cup salad oil
2 Tbsp. red wine vinegar
1 Tbsp. lemon juice
2 Tbsp. sugar
1/2 tsp. salt
1/2 tsp. dry mustard
1/2 tsp. grated onions
1 garlic bud, chopped
1 pkg. slivered almonds
1 large head romaine lettuce
1 can mandarin oranges, drained
2 or 3 chopped green onions

Combine salad oil, vinegar, lemon juice, sugar, salt, dry mustard, grated onion and garlic bud in shaker; refrigerate overnight.

Toast almonds about 30 minutes at 250°. This is a must — it makes a difference in taste.

Toss romaine lettuce, oranges, green onions and almonds with dressing at the last minute. Yield: 4 servings.

▲ ▲ ▲

Citrus salad

From Betty Finley, a Rutledge caterer.

3 Tbsp. raspberry vinegar
1/3 cup sugar
1 tsp. finely chopped onion
1/2 tsp. salt
1/2 tsp. dry mustard
1/2 cup oil

2 tsp. poppy seeds
3 cups torn leaf lettuce
3 cups Boston or bibb lettuce
2 grapefruit, peeled, sectioned
3 oranges, peeled, sectioned

In blender container or food processor bowl with metal blade, combine raspberry vinegar, sugar, onion, salt and mustard. Cover and process until blended. With machine running, add oil in a slow, steady stream. Process until thick and smooth. Add poppy seeds. Process a few seconds to blend.

Toss lettuces together. Divide onto serving plates. Arrange fruit on top. Serve with dressing. Yield: 6 servings.

▲ ▲ ▲

Mexican tossed salad

Mrs. Fred Smith, Knoxville, sends a recipe for Mexican tossed salad that she says is good served with hamburgers.

1 head lettuce, torn in bite-size pieces
1 (15-oz.) can kidney beans, drained
2 to 3 tomatoes, cut into wedges
1/2 cup sliced green onions
Salt, pepper to taste
1 cup shredded cheddar cheese
3 cups regular size corn chips, crushed
Russian or Catalina bottled dressing

Place lettuce in large bowl. Top with beans, tomatoes, onions, salt and pepper. Toss lightly. Sprinkle cheese, then corn chips over top. Pour on dressing just before serving. Yield: 6 to 8 servings.

▲ ▲ ▲

* Calico salad

Kay Rodgers, hostess of the executive dining room at First American Bank, Knoxville, makes this light salad.

4 oz. salad shell pasta or rotini
1/2 cup light French dressing
1 (15 1/2-oz.) can kidney beans, drained
1 cup shredded cheddar cheese
1 cup quartered cherry tomatoes or coarsely chopped home-grown tomatoes
1/2 cup chopped green pepper
1/4 cup finely chopped onion (preferably purple)
1 (4-oz.) can chopped green chilies, drained

Cook pasta according to package directions. Drain. Add French dressing to warm pasta. (Warm pasta absorbs the flavor better.) Add kidney beans, cheese, tomatoes, green pepper, onion and chilies to pasta and toss gently.
Serve chilled or at room temperature. Yield: about 6 cups.

▲ ▲ ▲

Macaroni salad

Bobbie Merritt of Dandridge says the secrets to macaroni salad are letting it marinate overnight and adding no salt until serving time.

1 (7-oz.) pkg. macaroni
1 or 2 cucumbers, peeled and diced
1/2 green pepper, chopped
2 carrots, chopped in blender
2 tomatoes, peeled and diced (1 red, 1 yellow, if possible)
1 tsp. grated onion
3 small stalks celery, chopped
Salad dressing (not mayonnaise) to moisten

Cook macaroni according to package directions; drain well; let cool. Combine ingredients in half-gallon glass jar. Seal and refrigerate overnight. Serve on lettuce. Add salt to taste just before serving.

▲ ▲ ▲

Spaghetti salad

Chris Christenberry of Knoxville offers a recipe for spaghetti salad.

1 (7-oz.) pkg. very thin spaghetti, cooked according to package directions
1 cup diced cucumbers
1 cup diced green peppers
1 cup diced onions
1 cup diced tomatoes
1 cup diced celery
1 cup diced carrots
1 jar McCormick's Salad Supreme seasoning mix
1 bottle Italian dressing

Combine ingredients; let set several hours before serving. Yield: 8 to 10 servings.

▲ ▲ ▲
Hot potato salad

Virginia (Mrs. Glyn) Bounds shares a favorite salad recipes. Hot potato salad, a recipe her mother-in-law gave her when she was married 50 years ago, is easy to make and may be served in a variety of ways. For a picnic, she made it, then molded it, chilled it and decorated it with hard-cooked eggs.

4 or 5 average size potatoes
2 Tbsp. butter
1/2 cup chopped onion
Salt, pepper to taste
1 egg
1 Tbsp. flour
1/2 cup sugar
1/2 cup vinegar
1/2 cup cream

Peel potatoes, cook and mash them (without milk). Add butter, chopped onion, salt and pepper to taste. Set aside.

Beat together the egg and flour. Add sugar, vinegar and cream and cook in saucepan until it thickens like a sauce. Pour over potatoes. Mix well. Serve hot or chilled. Yield: 6 to 8 servings.

▲ ▲ ▲
Sweet potato salad

Sarah Watson contributes a recipe for sweet potato salad.

2 lbs. sweet potatoes
2/3 cup mayonnaise
2 Tbsp. lemon juice
1 cup diced celery
2 Tbsp. diced sweet pickles
2 Tbsp. diced green peppers
2 Tbsp. diced onions
1/2 tsp. salt

Boil potatoes in their skins until barely tender. Cool. Remove skins and dice. Combine remaining ingredients to make dressing. Add the potatoes and toss to coat with dressing. Chill or serve at once. Yield: 4 servings.

▲ ▲ ▲
Spinach salad

From Suzanne Neal, News-Sentinel staff writer, comes a trendy salad.

2 lbs. fresh spinach, stems removed, torn in pieces
1 pkg. Pepperidge Farm herb stuffing mix or herb croutons
1 lb. bacon, cooked and crumbled
3 or 4 hard-cooked eggs
Fresh mushrooms

Dressing:
2/3 cup oil   2 tsp. prepared mustard
1/3 cup sugar   1 tsp. celery salt
1/3 cup vinegar   1 sweet onion, sliced

Combine salad ingredients. Mix dressing; drizzle over salad when
ready to serve. Yield: 8 servings.

▲ ▲ ▲
* Cranberry-orange relish

2 cups fresh cranberries, finely chopped
2 Tbsp. grated orange rind
1 medium orange, peeled, sectioned, seeded and chopped
1 medium green apple, cored and finely chopped
1/3 cup sugar
1/4 tsp. ground ginger
1/4 tsp. ground nutmeg

Combine all ingredients in a medium bowl, stir well. Cover and chill
overnight. Yield: 8 servings.

▲ ▲ ▲
Pineapple-orange salad

*Edwina Ralston, News-Sentinel assistant features editor, brought this salad (or
dessert) to an office luncheon and it was a favorite.*

1 small can mandarin oranges, drained
1 (4-oz.) can crushed pineapple, with juice
1 cup (1 can) coconut
1 cup sour cream
1 1/2 cups miniature marshmallows

Combine ingredients and refrigerate. Serve on lettuce leaves.

▲ ▲ ▲
Watergate salad

In answer to a request for Watergate salad, we received similar recipes from Kay Zinn of Kingston, Pearlie Frye of Powder Springs, Mrs. George Burns of Louisville, and Sarah Davis of Knoxville.

1 (9-oz.) carton whipped topping
1 (3-oz.) pkg. instant pistachio pudding
1 (15- or 16-oz.) can crushed pineapple with juice
1 cup miniature marshmallows
1/2 cup finely chopped pecans

Fold pudding mix into whipped topping. Add remaining ingredients and refrigerate. If desired, add maraschino cherries, cut in pieces — use 1 small jar, drained. Yield: 8 servings.

▲ ▲ ▲
Angel salad

Angel salad has graced the family's Thanksgiving and Christmas dinner tables as long as she can remember, writes Anna Williams of Maryville. "Why is it dubbed 'angel salad?' It's heavenly," she says.

2 (3-oz.) pkgs. lime gelatin
2 cups boiling water
1 (8-oz) can crushed pineapple
2 (3-oz.) pkgs. cream cheese
1 cup diced celery
1 (2-oz.) jar chopped pimentos
1 cup chopped pecans
1/2 pint whipping cream, whipped

In a 1 1/2-quart (oblong) dish, dissolve gelatin in boiling water and let cool. Drain crushed pineapple and discard liquid. Mash cream cheese and add pineapple, celery, pimentos and pecans. Fold this mixture into cooled gelatin and place dish in refrigerator until gelatin becomes thick, but not firmly jelled (about 1 1/2 hours). Fold in whipped cream. Yield: 12 servings.

▲ ▲ ▲

Blueberry salad

Idonna Bryson, News-Sentinel office manager, often brings this salad to The
News-Sentinel Christmas lunch.

2 (3-oz.) pkgs. black raspberry or blackberry gelatin
2 cups boiling water
1 cup fruit liquid (saved from drained berries and pineapple)
1 (15-oz.) can blueberries, drain and save liquid
1 (8-oz.) can crushed pineapple, drain and save liquid

Topping:
1 (8-oz.) pkg. cream cheese
1/2 cup sugar
1 (8-oz.) carton sour cream
1/2 tsp. vanilla
Chopped nuts (pecans or walnuts)

Dissolve gelatin, water and liquid saved from fruit. Add blueberries and
pineapple. Pour into 2-quart mold or dish. Refrigerate until firm. Blend
topping ingredients (except nuts), spread over gelatin mixture. Sprinkle
with chopped nuts. Yield: 10 to 12 servings.

▲ ▲ ▲

Cranberry salad

Bobbie Merritt of Dandridge sends a recipe she likes to use during the holidays.
She says she puts the cranberry salad in several dishes to give to friends.

1 large pkg. cherry gelatin
2 1/2 cups boiling water
1 bag cranberries, washed and drained
1 large or 2 small apples, diced
4 to 5 bananas, sliced
1 cup chopped nuts (optional)
1 cup sugar

Dissolve gelatin in boiling water and set aside. Chop cranberries in
blender and pour into serving bowl. Add apples, bananas, nuts and sugar.
Mix well and let set 10 minutes. Then add gelatin to fruit mixture.
Refrigerate in the serving bowl. Spoon out to serve. Yield: 8 servings.

▲ ▲ ▲
Grandma's salad

Karen Anne Woods, Knoxville, sends a recipe for a holiday salad from a TV show in Alaska. The gelatin mixture cannot be poured into a mold because it does not set up. Pour it into a serving dish and spoon it out, she says.

3 small pkgs. orange gelatin
1 cup boiling water
1 (No. 2) can (2 1/2 cups) crushed unsweetened pineapple, juice and all
3/4 cup sugar
1/2 lb. grated cheddar cheese
1 cup chopped nuts
2 pkgs. whipped topping mix (prepared) or 1 large carton whipped topping

Dissolve gelatin in boiling water. Bring pineapple and juice to a boil with the sugar. Add to gelatin mixture. Let set until the consistency of egg whites. Add cheddar cheese, nuts and whipped topping. Yield: 10 to 12 servings.

▲ ▲ ▲
Henry's heavenly hash

Ruth Sutton, who was hostess at the Laurel Room at the former Miller's department store, Knoxville, suggests heavenly hash from Chef Henry Hardy.

1 pkg. miniature marshmallows
9 egg whites, beaten until soft peaks form
9 egg yolks
3 (No. 10) cans fruit cocktail, drained overnight
1 1/2 cups sugar
1 cup lemon juice
4 Tbsp. unflavored gelatin
1 quart whipping cream
3 Tbsp. confectioners' sugar
1 cup chopped walnuts, optional

Combine sugar, egg yolks, and lemon juice and cook slowly until thickened. Add unflavored gelatin slowly. Let cool to room temperature. Whip cream, fold in confectioners' sugar. Fold all ingredients together easily (that is the secret — fold easily). Add walnuts, if desired.

This will serve 25 and will keep for several days. In fact, it is better when kept overnight.

▲ ▲ ▲
Heavenly hash

Graham crackers may be substituted for the vanilla wafers in this recipe.

1 (3-oz.) pkg. orange gelatin
1 cup boiling water
1 cup cold water
1/2 cup sugar
1 pint whipping cream, whipped
1/2 cup sugar
1/2 tsp. vanilla
1/2 cup finely chopped nuts
1 cup finely broken vanilla wafers
1 cup miniature marshmallows
1 cup drained crushed pineapple
1/2 cup shredded coconut

Dissolve gelatin in boiling water. Add cold water and 1/2 cup sugar. Stir well until sugar and gelatin are dissolved. Set aside to cool. Meanwhile whip cream, adding 1/2 cup sugar and vanilla to whipped cream. When gelatin has cooled, whip it with an egg beater. When mixture is very light, fold in whipped cream.

Add nuts, vanilla wafers, marshmallows, crushed pineapple and coconut. Mix well. Pour into mold and set in refrigerator several hours to chill. Serve in sherbet glasses. Yield: 8 to 10 servings.

▲ ▲ ▲
Purple lady salad

1 (6-oz.) pkg. red raspberry gelatin
1 cup hot water
1 (1-lb.) can blueberries (not drained)
1 (15 1/4-oz.) can crushed pineapple (not drained)
1 cup pecans, finely chopped
1/4 pint whipping cream, whipped

Dissolve gelatin in hot water, stir as necessary. Add blueberries with syrup. Add pineapple with liquid. Refrigerate until almost set, then stir in chopped nuts and whipped cream. Refrigerate until serving time. Yield: 8 servings.

▲ ▲ ▲
Ribbon congealed salad

Berniece Shamblin, Etowah, contributes a recipe for ribbon congealed salad.

1 (3-oz.) pkg. lemon gelatin	1 (3-oz.) pkg. cream cheese
1 (3-oz.) pkg. lime gelatin	2 1/2 Tbsp. mayonnaise
1 (3-oz.) pkg. cherry gelatin	· 1 small can crushed pineapple

In small bowl, dissolve lemon gelatin in 3/4 cup boiling water. Add cream cheese and mayonnaise and whip until smooth. Pour into salad mold and chill in refrigerator until firm. Dissolve cherry gelatin in 1 cup boiling water; add 1/2 cup ice cold water. When chilled, pour cherry gelatin on top of lemon layer and refrigerate until set. Dissolve lime gelatin in 3/4 cup boiling water and add pineapple, juice and all. Cool. When cherry layer is set, pour lime gelatin on top to form a third layer. Cover and chill. Unmold to serve. Yield: 8 to 10 servings.

▲ ▲ ▲
Blue cheese dressing

3 pkgs. blue cheese
1 pint Miracle Whip or mayonnaise
2 cartons sour cream
Dash sugar
Dash catsup
Dash Worchestershire sauce

Combine ingredients. Store in refrigerator.

▲ ▲ ▲
Cheddar cheese dressing

This is similar to the dressing served at Calhoun's restaurants, Knoxville.

1 1/2 cup mayonnaise
1/2 cup buttermilk
1/2 cup finely shredded cheddar cheese
Dash Worcestershire sauce
Dash red wine vinegar
Pinch each of salt, ground black pepper, ground red pepper

Combine all ingredients in medium bowl and blend thoroughly. Store in tight container in refrigerator.

▲ ▲ ▲

Coleslaw dressing

Sarah A. Russell of Speedwell sends this recipe for coleslaw dressing from the Little Tunnel Inn at Cumberland Gap. She got it in 1967.

2 cups sugar
1 cup white vinegar

1/2 cup water
Mayonnaise

Combine sugar, vinegar and water in saucepan. Cook 3 minutes after the mixture starts to boil. Remove from heat and taste. If it is sour, add a little more water and cook another 3 minutes. Cool. Add mayonnaise to taste when ready to combine with chopped cabbage.

▲ ▲ ▲

Creamy raspberry dressing

Fruit-flavored vinegars are wonderful to use in salad dressings and sauces. Caterer Betty Finley, Rutledge, sends this one using raspberry vinegar. Try this dressing on spinach salad. Wash spinach leaves and drain well. Combine with sliced fresh pear (red is pretty) and purple onion rings (three or four to a salad). Sprinkle with bright red pomegranate seeds.

1/3 cup oil
3 Tbsp. sugar
2 Tbsp. raspberry vinegar
1 Tbsp. sour cream
1 1/2 tsp. Dijon mustard
1/2 cup fresh raspberries or 1/2 cup frozen whole raspberries, without syrup, thawed

Combine ingredients. Store in glass jar in refrigerator.

▲ ▲ ▲

Dijon honey dressing

1 cup mayonnaise
1/4 cup Dijon mustard
1/4 cup vegetable oil
1/4 cup honey
Small pinch red pepper
1/8 tsp. onion salt
3/4 tsp. cider vinegar

Blend all ingredients together well. Refrigerate. Dressing will keep about 3 weeks; discard when oil starts to separate.

▲ ▲ ▲
Gourmet's Market vinaigrette

1/3 cup extra virgin olive oil

1 Tbsp. fine vinegar (raspberry, white wine, balsamic, champagne or sherry)

1/4 tsp. freshly ground black pepper

1/2 tsp. prepared Dijon mustard

1 tsp. fresh herbs (such as tarragon and basil) or 1/2 tsp. dried herbs moistened with 1/2 tsp. water

1 tsp. snipped fresh chives or minced shallots

Whisk all ingredients together. If a vinegar of high acidity is used, add 1/2 tsp. water. Lemon juice may be used instead of vinegar.

▲ ▲ ▲
Honey French dressing

1 cup vegetable oil

1/2 cup honey

1/2 cup catsup

1/3 cup vinegar

1/3 cup chopped onion

1 Tbsp. Worcestershire sauce

1/2 tsp. salt

Combine ingredients in blender. Yield: 2 2/3 cups.

▲ ▲ ▲
* Olive oil dressing
Ray Roman of Jefferson City makes an olive oil dressing.

1/2 cup extra virgin olive oil

1 Tbsp. balsamic vinegar or red wine vinegar

2 Tbsp. fresh lemon juice

1/4 tsp. oregano

1 garlic clove, chopped extra fine

Salt (optional)

Pepper (to taste)

Blend all ingredients in blender or with a wire whip. Yield: 2 servings.

▲ ▲ ▲

Barbecue sauce

Jerry and Patricia Jackson, who live in Cumberland, Pa., serve barbecue at large events because it can be easily doubled or tripled. Jerry's mother, Opal Jackson of Oliver Springs, says the recipe originated in a family cookbook. It is inexpensive to make.

1/4 cup vinegar
1/2 cup water
1/2 tsp. black pepper
Pinch cayenne pepper
1 Tbsp. prepared mustard
1 1/2 tsp. salt
1/4 cup butter
1 small onion, chopped
4 Tbsp. Worcestershire sauce
1 thick or 3 thin lemon slices
2 Tbsp. sugar (optional — to taste)
1/2 cup tomato sauce

Mix all ingredients except tomato sauce together and simmer for 20 minutes. Add tomato sauce, bring to a boil and remove from heat. Remove lemon slice, first squeezing it against side of pan to get juice out. When ready to serve, pour sauce over cooked beef, chicken or pork and reheat.
Sauce will keep in refrigerator for several weeks.

▲ ▲ ▲

Homer's barbecue sauce

Laura P. O'Callaghan of Knoxville offers this barbecue sauce.

2 lemons
2 sticks butter or margarine
3 cups vinegar
2 onions, chopped
2 garlic cloves, chopped
1 cup Heinz 57 sauce

1 cup catsup
4 tsp. dry mustard
4 tsp. sugar
Salt, pepper
1/3 cup Worcestershire sauce
1 tsp. Tabasco sauce

Squeeze lemons for the juice. Put juice and remaining lemon halves in sauce.
Combine ingredients and simmer for 1/2 hour. Baste meat with sauce the last half hour it cooks. Mix half the sauce with cut up meat. Serve remaining sauce in bowl to pour over meat, if desired.

▲ ▲ ▲

Chili sauce

Mary Chester, Norris, makes this sauce out of fresh tomatoes. She does not process the sauce, but the U.S. Department of Agriculture says to process pints of chili salsa (sauce) in boiling water bath for 20 minutes.

1 gallon ripe tomatoes
2 cups chopped onions
2 cups chopped sweet green peppers
1 cup sugar
3 Tbsp. salt
1 Tbsp. mustard seed
1 Tbsp. celery seed
3 Tbsp. mixed pickling spices
2 1/2 cups vinegar

Wash and drain vegetables. Scald, core, peel and chop tomatoes. Peel onions. Seed peppers. Chop onions and peppers. Mix all ingredients except spices and vinegar. Boil 45 minutes. Add spices, tied in bag made out of a small square of cheesecloth. Boil until very thick, then add vinegar and boil until mixture is as thick as wanted.

Taste. Add more seasoning and sugar, if desired. Remove spice bag and discard. Pour boiling hot sauce into hot canning jars. Seal at once.

Chester uses a wooden spoon to stir the sauce and if it begins to stick, she takes it off the heat. She likes to serve it on white beans with corn bread and on hot dogs.

▲ ▲ ▲

Teriyaki marinade

This teriyaki marinade is similar to the one served at Ruby Tuesday restaurants, Nancy Baker of Dandridge reports. Leftover sauce can be refrigerated.

1 cup pineapple juice
1 cup soy sauce
2 Tbsp. brown sugar
3 Tbsp. Worcestershire sauce
1 Tbsp. ground pepper
1 tsp. chopped garlic

Mix together. Marinate chicken in the mixture 24 hours before cooking on grill or marinate steaks 12 hours. Also use it as a basting sauce while chicken or beef is on the grill.

▲ ▲ ▲
* Zero-cholesterol hollandaise sauce

Cici Williamson and Ann Steiner, who write our MicroScope column, created this recipe.

1/2 cup egg substitute
2 Tbsp. fresh lemon juice
Pinch of cayenne pepper
1/3 cup margarine

Put egg substitute, lemon juice and cayenne pepper into a blender or food processor; blend. Put margarine into a 1-cup glass measuring cup. Cover and microwave on high 1 1/2 minutes or until boiling. Turn on blender and pour margarine through lid; blend. Sauce should thicken slightly. For additional thickening or reheating, pour sauce into same glass measure and microwave on high 10 seconds. Stir; repeat if necessary. Yield: 1 cup, 35 calories per tablespoon.

Breads and
sandwich spreads

▲ ▲ ▲

Breads and sandwich spreads

▲ ▲ ▲

Banana bread surprise

News-Sentinel staff writer Suzanne Foree Neal provides this recipe. It can be varied by reducing sugar by 1/4 cup and adding 1/2 to 2/3 of a small jar of preserves. Also, try cutting half of the banana and adding a cup of berries.

1 cup sugar	2 cups all-purpose flour
3 to 4 mashed ripe bananas	1/2 cup chopped nuts
1/2 cup softened butter (no substitute)	1 tsp. baking soda
1/4 cup milk	1/2 tsp. salt
1 tsp. vanilla	
2 eggs	

Blend first 6 ingredients with spoon until well mixed. Stir in remaining ingredients until just moistened. Pour into 9-by-5-inch loaf pan. Bake at 350° for 1 hour.

▲ ▲ ▲

Irish soda bread

Kay Bone, Knoxville, whose parents came to the U.S. from Ireland, prepared her authentic Irish soda bread for Annemarie Huste, director of a New York cooking school and former White House chef, when she was in Knoxville to teach cooking classes. The bread was a hit and Huste requested the recipe.

1 cup raisins	1 tsp. salt
5 cups flour	1 stick margarine
1 cup sugar	1 1/2 Tbsp. caraway seeds
2 tsp. baking powder	2 to 2 1/2 cups buttermilk
1 tsp. baking soda	1 egg, beaten

Plump raisins in hot water a couple of minutes, until soft. Drain.
Mix together flour, sugar, baking powder, soda and salt. Add margarine and work in well. Add caraway seeds, 1 cup buttermilk and beaten egg. Mix well. Add raisins and gradually add remaining buttermilk — enough to take up dry flour. (You may not need to use all the buttermilk.) Knead 1 minute. Place dough into 2 greased 9-by-5-inch loaf pans. Sprinkle additional sugar and add small pieces of margarine on top. Cut two lines across top of each loaf. (This will prevent bread from cracking.) Bake at 350° for 1 hour, or less, until well browned. Cool slightly on rack. Bread is best if served still warm.

▲ ▲ ▲

* Oatmeal raisin bread

Anabel McConnell of Kingsport, a retired physician, loves to bake yeast bread. This one is a healthy choice. McConnell sometimes adds wheat germ or bran to the whole wheat flour for increased fiber content —about 1/4 cup of wheat germ or bran in place of 1/4 cup of whole wheat flour.

1/2 cup whole wheat flour	1 pkg. dry yeast
1/2 cup packed dark brown sugar	1/2 cup warm water (105° to 115°)
1 tsp. salt	5 to 6 cups all purpose flour
1/2 cup butter or margarine, softened	1/2 cup sugar
1 cup quick cooking oats, uncooked	1 Tbsp. ground cinnamon
1 cup raisins	Melted butter
2 cups boiling water	

Combine first 6 ingredients in large bowl. Mix well. Add boiling water, stirring to melt butter. Cool to 105 to 115 degrees. (Use candy thermometer to measure.)

Dissolve yeast in 1/2 cup warm water. Let stand for 5 minutes. Add to oats mixture and mix well. Gradually stir in enough flour to make a soft dough. Turn dough out on floured surface and knead until smooth and elastic, 8 to 10 minutes. Place in a greased bowl, turning to grease the top. Cover and let rise 1 hour or until doubled in volume.

Punch dough down. Turn out on floured surface and knead for 2 minutes. Divide dough in half and let rest for 10 minutes. Roll each half into a rectangle 18-by-9-inches. Brush melted butter over each rectangle. Combine sugar and cinnamon. Sprinkle half over each rectangle. Roll each rectangle up, jelly roll fashion, beginning at a short 9-inch side. Fold under ends of rolls and place in two greased 9-by-5-by-3-inch loaf pans. Brush with melted butter and let rise, covered, for 40 to 50 minutes. Bake at 375° for 40 to 50 minutes. Remove from pans; cool on wire racks.

▲ ▲ ▲

Orange-cranberry bread

Linda Lange of Knoxville likes this bread during the holidays.

2 cups all purpose flour	1 egg, slightly beaten
1 cup sugar	2 Tbsp. margarine, melted
1 1/2 tsp. baking powder	2 Tbsp. hot water
1/2 tsp. salt	1 cup cranberries, chopped
1/2 tsp. baking soda	1/2 cup chopped nuts
1/2 cup orange juice	1 Tbsp. grated orange rind

Preheat oven to 350°. Combine dry ingredients. Mix together juice, egg, margarine and water. Add to dry ingredients, stirring until just blended. Fold in cranberries, nuts and orange rind. Pour into greased 9-by-5-inch loaf pan. Bake for 1 hour.

▲ ▲ ▲

Sourdough bread

Carol Taylor, Knoxville, offers sourdough bread from a recipe that originated with Helen McKinney. Another version of starter follows on the next page.

Starter:
1/2 cup regular beer (not "light")
1 tsp. dry yeast

3 Tbsp. instant potato flakes
1 cup warm (not hot) water
2/3 cup granulated sugar

Combine ingredients in a glass or plastic container (no metal). Cover loosely. Let mixture stand at room temperature all day, then refrigerate for 3 to 5 days.

To feed starter:
3/4 cup sugar

3 Tbsp. instant potato flakes
1 cup warm water

Combine ingredients. Add to starter. Let stand at room temperature, out of drafts, 8 to 12 hours. Shake occasionally throughout the day to re-mix. It will be bubbly. Use 1 cup to make bread and return the rest to the refrigerator. After 3 to 5 days, feed starter again. If you are not making bread, discard 1 cup of starter. You can feed starter two or three times before using any of it since this avoids depleting its fermentation power.

To make bread:
6 cups bread flour
1 tsp. granulated sugar
1 Tbsp. salt

1 1/2 cups warm water
1/2 cup oil
1 cup starter

In a large glass or plastic bowl (no metal), combine dry ingredients well. Add warm water, oil and the starter. Mix well with a wooden spoon (no metal) and then with your hands to make a stiff batter. Pour 2 tablespoons oil into large mixing bowl. Put the dough into the oiled bowl and rotate dough so the oiled side is up. Cover lightly with plastic wrap and let set at room temperature overnight. Do not refrigerate.

In the morning, punch down the bread 8 to 10 times. Divide the dough into thirds. Knead each 4 to 5 times on a floured surface.

To make bread: Shape into loaves. Put into three greased or non-stick 9-by-5-inch loaf pans. Brush top of loaves with oil, cover with a towel and let stand at room temperature 5 to 8 hours, depending on how warm the house is. (The bread rises more slowly if house is cool.)

To make dinner rolls: Pinch off sections of kneaded dough into balls the size of large eggs. Put three balls in each section of muffin tins for separated rolls or place balls together, touching each other, on a 9-by-13-inch pan or throw-away aluminum pans for pull-apart rolls. Let rise all day.

Bake loaves at 350° for 30 to 40 minutes or rolls 12 to 15 minutes. If desired, brush tops with margarine. Cool in pans on their sides on a rack.

Additional tips: Starter may be frozen. To bring it back, thaw it to room temperature, stir it and start as if it's day one.

To make wheat bread, use 2 cups wheat flour to 4 cups bread flour.

Jean Barn   Knoxville gives his version of water without beer.

1 pkg. yeast (regular, not rapid-rise)
1 cup warm water
3/4 cup sugar
3 Tbsp. instant potato flakes

Combine ingredients in jar. (It is not necessary to dissolve the yeast in warm water first). Cover loosely. Let mixture set on counter about 5 hours, until it ferments. Refrigerate in jar with lid on for three to five days.

▲ ▲ ▲

Spinach corn bread

Ruth Weber of Knoxville, who liked the spinach corn bread at Morningside Inn, Maryville, obtained the recipe from the chef. She then adapted it to family use.

2 boxes Jiffy corn bread mix
1 small box frozen chopped spinach, thawed and drained
1/2 cup melted margarine
6 eggs
1/2 cup cottage cheese

Combine ingredients. Pour into greased 9-by-13-inch pan. Bake at 350° for 30 to 35 minutes.

▲ ▲ ▲

Sweet potato bread

1/3 cup butter, softened
1 cup sugar
2 eggs, beaten
1/2 cup molasses
1 cup mashed sweet potatoes
1/4 cup raisins
3/4 cup chopped walnuts

2 cups sifted flour
1/4 tsp. baking powder
1 tsp. baking soda
1/2 tsp. salt
1/2 tsp. cinnamon
1/2 tsp. nutmeg
1/2 tsp. allspice
1/4 tsp. ground cloves

Preheat oven to 350°. Blend together the butter, sugar, eggs, molasses and sweet potatoes in a bowl. In another bowl, sift together the flour, baking powder, soda, salt, cinnamon, nutmeg, allspice and cloves. Combine the two mixtures, stirring until smooth. Add raisins and walnuts. Pour into a greased, medium loaf pan and bake 1 hour.

▲ ▲ ▲

Bran rolls

Johnnie Rodgers, New Market, makes these rolls.

1/2 cup shortening
1/4 cup sugar
1/2 cup All-Bran cereal
1 tsp. salt
1/2 cup boiling water

1 pkg. yeast
1/4 cup lukewarm water
1 egg, beaten
3 1/2 cups all-purpose flour

Pour boiling water over shortening, sugar, cereal and salt. Dissolve yeast in lukewarm water. Add egg to cereal mixture; cool to lukewarm. Add yeast mixture. Add flour and beat well. Place in bowl, cover and refrigerate at least 6 hours. Pat dough out on board. Cut out with floured biscuit cutter. Fold rolls in half and dip in melted butter. Place on greased pan. Let rise until double, about an hour. Bake at 400° for 15 minutes.

▲ ▲ ▲

Buttermilk rolls

Knoxville chef Kenneth Badgett makes these rolls.

3 pkgs. yeast
1/2 cup hot tap water
5 cups self-rising flour
1/4 cup sugar
1 cup solid shortening or 2 sticks margarine
1 tsp. soda
2 cups warm buttermilk
2 cups self-rising flour
1`or 2 sticks margarine, melted

Dissolve yeast in water. In large bowl, combine 5 cups flour and sugar. Work in shortening until crumbly. Warm buttermilk in saucepan. Holding pan over flour, dissolve soda in buttermilk. (It will foam up and may foam over into flour.) When it foams, pour buttermilk into flour. Add yeast. Stir until blended.

Add about 2 cups more flour, stirring until mixture comes away from bowl and makes a ball. Remove dough. Grease bowl with oil. Return dough to bowl and turn to coat all sides with oil. Cover bowl. Let dough rise 45 minutes to 1 hour.

Flour a board and knead dough until it stretches like elastic, about 5 minutes. Pat or roll dough to 1/4-inch thickness. Let rise 15 to 20 minutes. Cut with floured biscuit cutter. Melt margarine. Dip rolls in margarine, fold them in half and press edges together. Place on a greased pan. Let rolls rise again for 20 minutes. Bake at 375° for about 20 to 25 minutes or until golden brown. Watch carefully. When you take them out of oven, brush them again with melted margarine. Yield: 3 to 4 dozen rolls.

▲ ▲ ▲
Potato rolls

Nancy Cannon, assistant in the First American National Bank executive dining room, Knoxville, is well-known for her rolls.

2 pkgs. dry yeast
1 1/2 cups warm water
2/3 cup sugar
6 cups all-purpose flour
2/3 cup solid shortening
1 cup mashed potatoes (cooked potatoes mashed without milk or seasonings)
2 eggs
1 1/2 tsp. salt

Dissolve yeast in warm water with 1 teaspoon sugar added to it. Let stand for 5 minutes. Mix in 2 cups flour, shortening and mashed potatoes. Add eggs and remaining sugar. Add remaining 4 cups flour and salt. Let dough rise 1 hour, until double in size. Roll dough out to 1/2-inch thickness. With floured biscuit cutter, cut into 2-inch circles. Brush melted butter on circles, fold them over and brush butter on top. Place on lightly greased baking sheet. Let rise 1 hour. Bake at 375° for 15 minutes or until brown.

Note: The rolls may be prepared and left on baking sheet in refrigerator overnight or until ready to use.

▲ ▲ ▲
Sour cream and chive rolls

Rhonda Taylor, who headed one of the Elegant Dining for the Symphony series honoring the Knoxville Symphony Orchestra, made these rolls for a garden party luncheon.

1/2 cup butter, softened
1 (8-oz.) carton sour cream
2 cups Bisquick
3 Tbsp. chopped chives (fresh or freeze-dried)

Beat softened butter; stir in sour cream. Gradually add Bisquick, stirring just until moist. Add chives and spoon into lightly-greased miniature muffin tins, filling 2/3 full. Bake at 350° for 15 minutes. Yield: 3 dozen.

Note: Muffins may be made in regular-size tins. Bake 20 minutes at 350°. Will make 1 dozen.

▲ ▲ ▲
Spoon rolls

Helen Phillips, Newport, sends a recipe for spoon rolls. She says the dough keeps for several days so you can bake a few at a time and save rest of the dough in the refrigerator to use later.

1 pkg. dry yeast
2 cups very warm water
1 1/2 sticks margarine, melted
1/4 cup sugar
1 egg
4 cups self-rising flour

Place yeast in the 2 cups warm water. Melt margarine. Mix with sugar in large bowl. Add beaten egg. Add dissolved yeast. Stir in flour until well mixed. Place in air tight bowl and keep in refrigerator. To cook, drop by spoonfuls into well-greased muffin tins. Bake at 350 to 400° for 20 minutes, or until brown. Yield: 2 dozen rolls.

▲ ▲ ▲
Whole wheat rolls

Bill Orr of Jefferson City makes rolls that are light in flavor and texture. He uses part whole wheat flour, but all white flour may be used.

1 Tbsp. sugar
2 pkgs. dry yeast
1/2 cup warm water
2/3 cup solid shortening
1/2 cup sugar

1 tsp. salt
1 cup scalded milk
2 eggs, well beaten
4 cups all-purpose flour
1 cup whole wheat flour

Dissolve the 1 tablespoon sugar and yeast in warm water. Combine shortening, 1/2 cup sugar, salt and scalded milk in saucepan so shortening will melt. Cool. Pour mixture into large bowl. With electric beater, add eggs. Add the whole wheat flour and about 1 cup of the all-purpose flour. When mixture starts to get hard to beat with the mixer, add the yeast mixture. Add remaining flour, cover and let rise about 1 to 1 1/2 hours. (If you want to hold the rolls until the next day, refrigerate overnight. It will rise on its own.)

Knead dough several times. Roll or pat dough out on floured board to about 1/4-inch thickness. Cut with floured biscuit cutter. Dip in melted butter. Fold rolls in half and place on greased pan. Let rise about 1 hour.

Bake at 350° for 10 to 12 minutes, until very light brown. Yield: 60 rolls.

▲ ▲ ▲

Fast food biscuits

Chris Bryant, Johnson City, sends a recipe for biscuits similar to those served at Hardee's restaurants.

4 cups self-rising flour
2 Tbsp. sugar
3 Tbsp. baking powder
7 Tbsp. solid shortening
2 cups buttermilk

Sift flour, sugar and baking powder together. Cut shortening into flour mixture. Mix in buttermilk with a fork, just until dough is moistened. Form large ball. Place on floured surface and knead a few times. Roll out about 3/4-inch thick and cut with large (3-inch) biscuit cutter. Place on greased baking sheet with sides of biscuits touching each other. Bake at 450° about 15 minutes, until brown.

The prepared biscuits may be frozen, wrapped tightly in foil. When ready to reheat, loosen foil and bake at 350° about 10 minutes.

▲ ▲ ▲

Rhett Butler's biscuits

Where the name originated, we don't know, but the recipe for Rhett Butler's biscuits is often requested. Ora Gault and Jeanette Cradic, both of Knoxville, share this:

2 pkgs. yeast
1/4 cup lukewarm water
5 cups self-rising flour
1/3 cup sugar
1 cup shortening
2 cups buttermilk
1 stick butter, melted

Dissolve yeast in lukewarm water. Sift together flour and sugar. Cut shortening into flour mixture. Add yeast and buttermilk. Mix well. Chill 1 hour.

Roll dough out 1/2-inch thick on floured surface. Cut into biscuits and place on greased pan. Cover with damp cloth and set aside to rise 1 hour in a warm place. Bake at 350° for 15 minutes. Brush with melted butter as biscuits begin to brown. Continue to bake until biscuits are a golden brown.

▲ ▲ ▲
Twins Cafe biscuits

Twins Hassie Seivers and Lassie Disney, former owners of Twins Cafe, Clinton, were featured on Good Morning America television show. The twins are famous for their biscuits, and they say they made more than 2 1/2 million of them through their careers at the cafe. They used lard rather than vegetable shortening and added baking powder to self-rising flour because they prepared the biscuits 30 minutes before baking them to give them a smooth appearance on top.

2 cups self-rising flour
2 tsp. baking powder
1/4 cup lard
3/4 cup buttermilk

Combine flour and baking powder. Cut lard into flour with pastry blender or fork, until mixture resembles coarse crumbs. Blend in buttermilk with a fork. On lightly floured surface, knead dough gently 10 to 12 times. Roll out dough and cut with floured biscuit cutter. Place on greased pan and let set 30 minutes. Bake at 450° until biscuits rise. Place under broiler and let brown.

▲ ▲ ▲
Angel corn muffins

Mrs. H. Roy Reams, Morristown, contributes the recipe for these light cornmeal muffins.

1 cup self-rising cornmeal
1 cup self-rising flour
1 pkg. yeast
1 Tbsp. sugar
1/2 tsp. soda
2 eggs, beaten
1/2 cup corn oil
1 1/2 cups buttermilk

Mix dry ingredients together. Add eggs, oil and buttermilk. Bake in greased muffin pans for 12 to 15 minutes at 450°.

▲ ▲ ▲

Applesauce muffins

This recipe is from Ann Stubblefield.

1 cup sugar
1/2 cup butter or margarine
1 egg
1 cup applesauce
1 tsp. soda
2 cups flour
1/2 tsp. cinnamon
1 1/2 tsp. allspice
1 Tbsp. vanilla
Confectioners' sugar

Beat together the butter and sugar. Add egg and beat. Heat applesauce and stir soda into it. Add to sugar mixture. Add sifted flour, spices and vanilla to creamed mixture, mixing well. Pour into greased or paper-lined muffin tins and bake at 350° until brown, 15 to 20 minutes. Sprinkle with confectioners' sugar. Yield: 18 to 20 medium-sized muffins.
    Note: Batter may be stored in refrigerator.

▲ ▲ ▲

Big Orange muffins

Karen Childs of Atlanta, formerly of Knoxville, suggests Big Orange muffins for a Vol football brunch.

2 cups sifted all-purpose flour
1/2 cup sugar
1 Tbsp. baking powder
1/2 tsp. salt
2 eggs, beaten
1/2 cup melted butter or margarine
1/2 cup orange juice (include pulp, if available)
2 Tbsp. grated orange rind

Preheat oven to 400°. Grease bottom of 12 muffin pan cups or line with paper liners. Sift flour, sugar, baking powder and salt into a bowl. Combine eggs, melted butter, orange juice and orange rind. Make a well in the center of the flour mixture. Pour in liquid ingredients all at once. Mix very lightly, just until dry ingredients are moistened. Batter will be lumpy. Fill muffin cups 2/3 full. Bake 20 to 25 minutes, or until lightly browned.
    Serve hot with butter, honey or orange marmalade.

▲ ▲ ▲
Blueberry muffins

Betty Barkley, former executive chef at Valley Fidelity Bank, now First Tennessee Bank, Knoxville, made these muffins when Valley had its executive dining room.

1 3/4 cups all-purpose flour
1/2 cup sugar
2 1/2 tsp. baking powder
3/4 tsp. salt
1/4 cup chopped pecans
1 egg, slightly beaten
3/4 cup milk
1/3 cup corn oil
1 cup fresh or frozen blueberries, thawed
2 Tbsp. sugar

Combine flour, 1/2 cup sugar, baking powder and salt in bowl. Add nuts. Combine egg, milk and oil. Add liquid mixture to dry mixture, stirring just until dry ingredients are moistened. Set aside. Toss berries with 2 tablespoons sugar and fold into batter. Spoon into regular-size, greased muffin tins, filling each about 2/3 full. Bake at 400° for 18 minutes or until golden brown.

▲ ▲ ▲
Ginger muffins

Ginger muffins were a popular item served at Knoxville's Buster Muggs restaurant, which was in the building now occupied by Calhoun's on the River. Ruth Weber's similar version may be cut in half. The muffins freeze well.

4 cups all-purpose flour
2 tsp. soda
1 tsp. salt
2 1/2 tsp. ginger
1/2 tsp. cinnamon
2 tsp. ground allspice

1 1/4 cups shortening
1 cup sugar
4 eggs
1 cup molasses
1 cup buttermilk
3/4 cup finely chopped nuts

Heat oven to 350°. Line with paper baking cups or grease 36 muffin cups. Lightly spoon flour into measuring cup; level off. In medium bowl, combine flour, soda, salt, ginger, cinnamon and allspice. Mix well.

In large bowl, beat together shortening and sugar. Beat until fluffy. Add eggs, molasses and buttermilk. Blend well. Stir in dry ingredients, just until moistened. Stir in nuts. Spoon batter into prepared muffin cups, filling 2/3 full. Bake for 20 to 25 minutes or until toothpick inserted in center comes out clean. Immediately remove from pans. Serve warm. Yield: 36 muffins.

▲ ▲ ▲

Meat salad sandwich filling

*Meat salad sandwich filling was served at Central High School in the 1940s.
The filling originated with the late Mary Hunter, who was Central's cafeteria
manager. Former students at Central often request the recipe.*

1 lb. ground beef
2 raw carrots, ground
1 raw green pepper, ground
1 raw onion, ground
Mayonnaise to desired consistency

Brown beef and drain well. When cool, mix with ground vegetables.
Combine with mayonnaise to make a spread for bread or rolls. Heat
under broiler, if desired.
    The filling should be served immediately, preferably at room
temperature. If it must be held, refrigerate.

▲ ▲ ▲

Ham salad spread

*News-Sentinel public service director Susan Alexander never liked ham salad
until she tried her mother-in-law's version.*

1 lb. Eckridge minced ham (no substitutes)
1 (2-oz.) jar pimentos, chopped
1 small onion
2 eggs, hard-cooked
2 heaping Tbsp. sweet pickle relish
Black pepper to taste
Equal parts mayonnaise and Miracle Whip to desired consistency

Grind ham, onion and eggs. Add pimentos, pickle relish, and pepper.
Moisten with mayonnaise and Miracle Whip (about 1/2 cup each). Chill.

▲ ▲ ▲

School boy sandwich spread

The food service department of the former Knoxville City Schools provided this old-time recipe for school boy sandwich spread when a reader requested it for her husband. He said it was one of his favorite foods at West High School.

1 lb. ground beef
1 small onion, chopped fine
1 small can tomato sauce or 2 1/2 cups tomatoes, mashed
Salt to taste
Bread

Saute onion in small amount of oil. Add ground beef, stirring to break up. When brown, add tomato sauce or tomatoes and salt. Pinch off bread and add until moisture is absorbed. You want this so it can be spooned onto a bun, but is not runny. Serve on heated buns.

▲ ▲ ▲

Imperial salad spread

Vegetable spreads are popular today, but actually they were served many, many years ago, too. Benton McKeehan of Knoxville, whose father, the late C.B. McKeehan worked with the late T.E. Burns and later became president of T.E. Burns and Co., sends a recipe for imperial salad spread. The sandwich filling was a favorite at the long-ago grocery that was located at the corner of Market and Wall streets. It can be made without boiled ham or bologna.

1 large can pimentos
6 lbs. cabbage
1 medium onion
3 large cucumbers
3 green sweet peppers
2 red sweet peppers
2 lbs. boiled ham (or bologna)
1/2 cup mixed sweet pickle
Salt, pepper
1 pint mayonnaise

Mash pimento finely with fork. Put cabbage, onion, cucumbers, peppers, ham or bologna, pimento and sweet pickles through food chopper. Grind finely. Season with salt and pepper to taste. Mix with mayonnaise to make it spreadable.

▲ ▲ ▲

Pimento cheese spread

Marie Burnett, Knoxville, makes a wonderful pimento cheese spread.

10 oz. sharp cheddar cheese
Large jar pimentos, drained (reserve juice)
1/2 tsp. salt
1 heaping Tbsp. mayonnaise

Grate cheese and let it set at room temperature so it will be smooth. Add pimentos, salt, and stir in mayonnaise. Add some of the pimento juice to make it spread easily.

Note: Juice from sweet pickles may be used instead of pimento juice, if desired.

▲ ▲ ▲

Parmesan onion spread

Susan Alexander likes to spread this on rye bread and broil it. It makes a good appetizer when party rye is used.

1 small onion, finely chopped
1/2 cup grated Parmesan cheese
1 cup mayonnaise

Combine ingredients. Spread generously on rye bread and broil until brown and bubbly.

▲ ▲ ▲

Cream cheese and pecans

This filling is a favorite of retired features staffer Christine Anderson.

1 (8-oz.) pkg. cream cheese
1/2 cup chopped pecans
1/2 cup celery (optional)
Mayonnaise or milk, to thin

Combine cream cheese and pecans. Add celery, if desired. Thin to spreading consistency with mayonnaise and/or milk. Spread on whole wheat bread or on trimmed bread for party sandwiches.

▲ ▲ ▲

Cucumber cream cheese

2 (3-oz.) or 1 (8-oz.) pkg. cream cheese, softened
1 cucumber, peeled, seeds removed and grated
1 onion, grated
Salt to taste
1/8 tsp. hot pepper sauce
Mayonnaise

Combine ingredients, adding mayonnaise until spread is the desired consistency.

▲ ▲ ▲

Egg salad spread

4 eggs, hard-cooked
1 celery stalk, chopped
3 Tbsp. or more mayonnaise
1/2 tsp. salt
Pinch of pepper
1 Tbsp. sweet pickle relish

Peel and mash eggs in a small mixing bowl. Add mayonnaise, salt, pepper, celery and pickle relish. Chill in refrigerator.

Vegetables

WHEN CAVEMAN FIRST BASHED CAVEWOMAN.

▲ ▲ ▲
Vegetables

▲ ▲ ▲

Parmesan vegetables

Mrs. S.K. Causseaux, Knoxville, shares a recipe for a vegetable casserole.

1 pkg. frozen baby lima beans
1 can water chestnuts, drained (optional)
1 can mushrooms, drained (optional)
1 (1-lb.) can French cut green beans, drained
1 (1-lb.) can small peas, drained
1 cup mayonnaise or sour cream
1 cup Parmesan cheese
1 Tbsp. Worcestershire sauce
1/2 cup milk

Cook frozen limas until tender and drain well. Combine limas with other drained vegetables. Combine mayonnaise or sour cream, Parmesan, milk and Worcestershire sauce and fold into vegetables. Pour into casserole and bake at 350° for 20 minutes. Yield: 8 to 10 servings.

▲ ▲ ▲

* Potage of fresh vegetables

Richard ReMine of Knoxville offers a recipe for a vegetable mixture.

1 turnip, peeled and diced
1 celery stalk, diced
1 yellow onion, peeled and diced
1 carrot, peeled and diced
1 Irish potato, peeled and diced
1 small bunch of fresh chives, finely minced
1/2 rutabaga, peeled and diced (optional)
Dash black pepper
1/4 tsp. margarine (optional)

Prepare vegetables and place in kettle. Cover with cold water. Add pepper and margarine, if desired. Cook until tender, about 8 to 10 minutes, over moderate heat. Yield: 2 to 4 servings.

▲ ▲ ▲

* Vegetable corn bread bake

Christine Kahn, Knoxville, offers this fresh vegetable and corn bread casserole.

2 medium zucchini, sliced, about 2 to 2 1/2 cups
1 small eggplant, peeled and cubed (about 1 1/2 cups)
1 medium onion, sliced (about 1 cup)
1/4 cup olive or vegetable oil, divided
1 (14 1/2-oz.) can whole tomatoes
2 Tbsp. all-purpose flour
2 tsp. Italian seasoning
1 tsp. seasoned salt
1 cup self-rising cornmeal
1/4 cup milk
1 egg

Preheat oven to 425° and lightly grease an 8- or 9-inch glass casserole dish. Combine zucchini, eggplant, onion and 2 Tbsp. oil in dish and cover with plastic wrap. Vent one corner. Microwave on high 5 minutes or saute in oil in skillet. Mix tomatoes (including liquid and tomatoes, chopped), flour and spices. Stir into vegetables, cover and microwave or saute 5 more minutes. Pour into baking dish if sauteed in skillet.

Stir cornmeal, milk, egg and 2 Tbsp. oil until smooth. Pour evenly over vegetables. Bake uncovered 25 to 30 minutes or until corn bread is golden. Yield: 6 servings.

▲ ▲ ▲

* Vegetable-cheese stir-fry

1 Tbsp. vegetable oil
2 garlic cloves, finely minced
3 cups fresh vegetables: onions, carrots, string beans, mushrooms, broccoli, cauliflower or others, sliced evenly or bite-size
Salt, pepper to taste
3 Tbsp. white wine
2 chopped ripe tomatoes
1/3 pound Muenster cheese slices (or any cheese)

Heat vegetable oil in large skillet, then lightly brown the garlic. Add vegetables (except tomatoes) and stir-fry over medium high heat about 5 minutes. The vegetables should still be firm and at the height of their color when ready. Salt and pepper to taste. Add tomatoes and wine. Simmer a couple of minutes. Top with cheese. Place under a broiler until the cheese is melted and lightly browned. Serves 2 or 3 as a main course.

▲ ▲ ▲

Asparagus casserole

Dot Orr, Jefferson City, makes this easy asparagus casserole.

2 medium cans asparagus spears, drained
1/2 cup sour cream
1/2 cup mayonnaise
1 cup grated sharp cheddar cheese
1 cup crushed cheese crackers
Butter or margarine

Lay asparagus spears in a baking dish. Combine sour cream and mayonnaise and spread over asparagus. Sprinkle with cheese, then with crushed cheese crackers that have been mixed with small amount of melted butter or margarine. Bake at 350° for 20 to 25 minutes. Yield: 4 to 6 servings.

▲ ▲ ▲

Asparagus with orange-lemon sauce

1 bunch asparagus (2 to 2 1/2 lbs.)
1/4 lb. butter or margarine
1/4 cup fresh orange juice
4 tsp. fresh lemon juice
1/2 tsp. grated lemon rind
1/2 tsp. grated orange rind

Break off asparagus stalks as far down as they snap easily. Wash. Cook, covered, in small amount of boiling salted water until just tender. Drain, if necessary.

Melt butter or margarine. Stir in remaining ingredients. Heat to serving temperature, stirring occasionally. Serve with cooked asparagus. Garnish with lemon slices as desired. Yield: About 6 servings.

▲ ▲ ▲

Carol's asparagus casserole

*Carol Teeter of Clarksville likes to take this casserole to church suppers. The
Teeters are commercial asparagus growers.*

8 slices white bread
1 lb. steamed fresh asparagus, cut in pieces
1 1/2 cups shredded cheese (American or other favorite)
4 eggs
2 1/2 cups milk
1 1/2 tsp. salt
1/8 tsp. pepper
2 Tbsp. minced fresh onion
2 Tbsp. melted butter

Remove crusts from bread slices and cut bread into cubes. Arrange
half the bread in bottom of 10-by-6-by-2-inch baking dish (or any similar
dish). Cover with steamed asparagus pieces. Sprinkle cheese over
asparagus and cover with remaining bread. Beat eggs slightly and add
remaining ingredients. Pour over asparagus mixture in dish. Let stand 20
minutes. Bake 45 minutes at 325°, until puffy and lightly browned. Yield: 4
servings.

▲ ▲ ▲

Green beans

Knoxville chef Kenneth Badgett says his green bean recipe is quick and easy.

2 (16-oz.) cans French style green beans
2 Tbsp. butter
1 tsp. Praise Allah seasoning
1/4 tsp. salt
Dash pepper
1/2 cup zesty Italian dressing

Combine green beans in liquid with butter, Praise Allah, salt and
pepper and bring to a boil. Turn heat to low and let beans heat thoroughly,
about 20 minutes. Drain off most of liquid. Add Italian dressing. Serve hot.
Yield: 4 servings.

▲ ▲ ▲
Baked beans

DeeDee Booher, News-Sentinel editorial assistant, often takes baked beans with
sausage to potluck gatherings and it's always popular.

1 lb. sausage (hot or mild)
4 (8-oz.) cans pork and beans
1 large onion, chopped
1/2 cup (or more) barbecue sauce
1/2 cup ketchup
1 Tbsp. mustard

1/4 cup brown sugar
1 Tbsp. sausage drippings
1 Tbsp. Worcestershire sauce
1 clove garlic, minced
1 tsp. oregano
1/2 cup celery, chopped

Cook sausage and drain on paper towels or in a colander. Combine
ingredients. Pour into 9-by-13-inch casserole. Bake at 350° for 45 minutes
to 1 hour. Check and make sure they aren't getting too dry; if they tend to
become dry, add more barbecue sauce.
    If you use hot sausage, don't use hot barbecue sauce. Yield: 8 to 10
servings.

▲ ▲ ▲
Mixed bean bake

From Johanna Parkins, Morristown.

1/2 lb. bacon
1 large onion, chopped
1/4 cup green pepper, chopped
1 1/2 Tbsp. oil
2 (16-oz.) cans pork and beans (do not drain)
1 (16-oz.) can kidney beans, drained and rinsed
1 (16-oz.) can lima beans, drained and rinsed
1/3 cup (scant) firmly packed brown sugar
1/4 cup vinegar
1/2 cup catsup
1/2 cup chili sauce
1 tsp. dry mustard
1 Tbsp. Worcestershire sauce

Cook bacon until crisp; drain on paper towels and crumble. Drain pan
of grease. Saute onion and green pepper in vegetable oil. Combine
ingredients. Spoon into lightly greased casserole. Bake at 350° for 30 to
45 minutes. Yield: 8 to 12 servings.

▲▲▲

Broccoli casserole

Broccoli casserole is always popular and Christine Anderson, retired News-Sentinel fashion and travel editor, offers a favorite, flavored with blue cheese.

2 pkg. frozen chopped broccoli
2 Tbsp. butter
2 Tbsp. all-purpose flour
1 (3-oz.) pkg. cream cheese, softened

1 pkg. blue cheese, crumbled
1 cup milk
1/3 cup cracker crumbs

Cook broccoli long enough to thaw and break apart. Drain well. In saucepan melt butter. Blend in flour to make a smooth mixture. Add cheeses. Add milk and cook, stirring, until mixture comes to a boil. Add broccoli. Pour into 1-quart casserole and top with cracker crumbs. Bake at 350° for 30 minutes. Yield: 8 servings.

▲▲▲

* Carrot casserole

The two recipes below are from Sharon Miller of Knoxville.

8 carrots, sliced julienne
2 Tbsp. grated onion
2 Tbsp. horseradish
1/2 cup mayonnaise

1 tsp. salt
1/4 tsp. pepper
1/3 cup buttered crumbs

Cook carrots in salted water until tender. Drain. Mix all ingredients; put in greased casserole. Bake at 375° for 15 minutes. Yield: 6 servings.

▲▲▲

* Celery amandine

2 Tbsp. butter, divided
3/4 cup almonds
4 cups diagonally sliced, 2-inch pieces of celery
1 Tbsp. granulated chicken bouillon
1/2 tsp. garlic powder
2 tsp. onion flakes
2 Tbsp. dry white wine
1 tsp. parsley

Melt 1 tablespoon butter in skillet; add almonds and brown, stirring often. Remove almonds and set aside. Put remaining 1 tablespoon butter in skillet and add celery, bouillon granules, garlic powder and onion flakes. Cover and cook over medium heat until celery is tender-crisp. Stir in wine, almonds and parsley. Cook 3 minutes; serve at once. Yield: 6 servings.

▲ ▲ ▲
Deviled corn

Marshall and Shirley McGhee of Caryville send the two recipes below to use when fresh corn is available. He says his mother used them as long as she lived.

3 cups fresh corn, cooked
3 Tbsp. butter or margarine
1 tsp. prepared mustard
1/2 tsp. salt
Pepper to taste
3 Tbsp. grated mild cheese

Heat corn in butter. Add mustard, salt and pepper. Add cheese. Serve hot. Yield: 6 to 8 servings.

▲ ▲ ▲
Fresh cut (fried) corn

5 or 6 ears of corn (yellow or white)
Salt to taste (about 1 1/2 tsp.)
1 tsp. black pepper
1/2 cup flour
1 cup water
1/4 cup bacon drippings or shortening
1/2 stick margarine

Cut corn off the cob, about half the thickness of the kernel, then scrape cob. Add salt, pepper, flour. Mix with 1 cup of water. (If too thick, add more water as the corn cooks.)

Pour corn mixture into a hot skillet that contains bacon drippings or shortening. As corn cooks, add margarine. Cook on medium heat until corn bubbles, stirring constantly, as corn is thickened. Reduce heat to low. Let cook for about 30 minutes, stirring often.

A crust will form around and on the bottom of the skillet. Yield: 4 to 6 servings.

▲ ▲ ▲

Mustard greens in sour cream

From the University of Tennessee Extension Service comes this recipe.

1 lb. fresh mustard greens
1/2 tsp. salt
Pinch black pepper
1 1/2 tsp. fresh lemon juice
1 cup sour cream

Wash mustard greens thoroughly and cut off tough stems. Place in a saucepan with only the water that clings to the leaves. Cook over low heat 7 to 10 minutes or until tender. Lift cover frequently during the first part of cooking. Add remaining ingredients; toss gently to blend and heat only until hot. Yield: 4 to 5 servings.

▲ ▲ ▲

* Stewed greens

Barbara Perkins of Knoxville likes to cook a mixture of kale, turnip and mustard greens. After washing them several times, she removes the leaves from the stems. "Take your thumb and go down the stem and the leaf will come off," she says. She enjoys eating the raw stems she's cut off like celery.

Kale, turnip and mustard greens
Bacon drippings
Butter or margarine
Salt and pepper to taste

Cover the washed greens with water, bring to a boil and cook about 3 minutes. Pour the water off. (Some people prefer to cook the greens as long as an hour before pouring the water off.) Chop greens and put in a skillet with small amount of bacon drippings, butter or margarine and salt and pepper. Do not add any more water. Cook a few minutes, just until tender.

▲ ▲ ▲

* Turnip greens with corn dodgers

3 qts. cold water
1/4 lb. seasoning meat
Salt to taste
2 lbs. cleaned young turnip greens

Add seasoning meat to cold water and boil 45 minutes. Add greens and boil 1 hour. Drain and save liquid from greens. Chop and place on platter. Keep greens warm.

For corn dodgers:
1 cup self-rising white cornmeal
1/4 cup all-purpose flour
1/2 tsp. salt
1 small onion, finely chopped
2 Tbsp. melted margarine

Mix together cornmeal, flour, salt, onion and melted margarine. Add enough hot turnip greens pot liquor to form dough. Shape into hush puppy-sized balls and drop into boiling pot liquor. Reduce heat and cook in tightly-covered pot 20 to 25 minutes. Arrange dodgers around greens and pour remaining liquid (which will have thickened) over greens and dodgers. Yield: 4 servings.

▲ ▲ ▲

* Okra, corn and tomatoes

Phyllis Rainwater, Dandridge, makes a wonderful okra stir-fry in summer when vegetables are fresh. It can easily be increased in proportions you prefer.

1 large onion, chopped (or more to taste)
2 Tbsp. butter
3 tomatoes (or more), peeled, quartered and seeds removed
2 cups sliced fresh okra
2 cups fresh corn, cut off the cob
Salt, pepper to taste

Stir-fry chopped onions in butter. Add tomatoes and cook about 10 minutes. Add layer of okra, then layer of corn. Do not stir at this point. Cover with lid and cook about 20 minutes. Remove lid and stir. Season to taste with salt and pepper and serve. Yield: 3 to 4 servings.

▲ ▲ ▲

Okra and corn in cream

Rena Wright, Oak Ridge, sends a recipe for a dish using okra and corn.

1/4 cup margarine
1 1/2 cups uncooked corn, fresh or frozen
2 cups fresh or frozen okra, cut in 1/2-inch slices
1 tsp. salt
Dash of pepper
1/2 cup light cream

Heat margarine in 9-inch skillet. Add corn. Cook over low heat until just beginning to brown. Add okra, cover tightly and cook over very low heat for 10 minutes, stirring occasionally. Remove cover, sprinkle with salt and pepper. Add cream. Cook, stirring, until heated. Yield: 4 servings.

▲ ▲ ▲

Fried okra

1 lb. fresh okra
1/2 cup cornmeal
1/4 cup flour
Salt, pepper to taste

Wash and drain okra on paper towels. Cut off caps and stem ends and cut crosswise into 1/2-inch slices. Mix together cornmeal, flour, salt and pepper. (Use more or less flour, to taste.) Coat okra with flour mixture.

Heat 1/2-inch vegetable oil in skillet over medium-high heat. Test to be sure oil is hot enough by adding one piece of okra. If it sizzles, add the floured okra in batches. Leave enough room in the pan to turn the okra without layering it. Brown lightly on both sides, stirring occasionally. Don't turn okra too soon or flour-cornmeal mixture will fall to the bottom of the pan and burn. Remove okra and drain on paper towels. If necessary, drain the oil out of the skillet and wipe the bottom of the pan clean. Pour drained oil back into pan and repeat with second batch. Yield: 4 servings.

▲ ▲ ▲

Creamed peas in cheese ring

*Barbara Asbury, News-Sentinel Neighbors editor, makes an attractive vegetable
dish — creamed peas in a cheese ring — for holiday entertaining.
She says her late aunt, Hazel Asbury, from whom she got the recipe, used to
serve it with the peas inside the ring, but Barbara Asbury says she likes to serve
them side-by-side because the peas tend to get the inside of the ring a little
soggy. If your ring mold has a large enough center, put the peas in a bowl and
set it inside the ring.*

2 cans English peas
2 Tbsp. margarine
3/4 cup milk
2 heaping Tbsp. flour
Pepper to taste

Drain the peas, reserving the liquid in a cup. Heat peas in saucepan
over low heat. (Do not get too hot or they will pop.) Melt margarine in
another saucepan, add flour and whisk or stir to blend well. Gradually stir
in milk, stirring constantly to make sauce-like mixture. Add pepper. Add to
peas. If too thick, add a little of the reserved liquid until it is consistency
you like.

Cheese ring:
1 lb. cheddar cheese
1 cup cracker crumbs or cornflake crumbs
1 large can pimentos
3 eggs
1/4 tsp. salt
1/2 cup sugar
1 cup milk
1/2 cup lemon juice
1 tsp. mustard

Grind cheese and crackers in food processor or chopper. Add slivered
pimentos.

Beat eggs slightly in top of a double boiler. Add salt, sugar, milk, lemon
juice and mustard to egg mixture. Set top of double boiler over bottom part
of double boiler that has hot water and cook until egg mixture is light in
color and thickened. Pour over cheese mixture.

Grease a ring mold and dust it lightly with cracker crumbs. Pour
mixture into the ring mold and bake at 325° for 1 hour. Cool slightly before
removing from mold. Serve with creamed peas. Yield: 8 servings.

▲ ▲ ▲
* Oven sliced potatoes

4 Idaho potatoes, thinly sliced, but not peeled
1/4 cup butter or margarine
1 Tbsp. grated onion
1 tsp. salt
1/8 tsp. pepper

In a large shallow greased baking dish, arrange potato slices in layers.
In a small saucepan, melt butter. Add grated onion, salt and pepper. Brush
potato slices with butter mixture. Bake in 425° oven for 1 hour or until
potatoes are crisp and brown.
Yield: 4 to 6 servings.

▲ ▲ ▲
Potato fingers

1/4 cup butter or margarine
1/2 cup chopped onion
1/4 cup chopped red pepper
1/4 cup grated Parmesan cheese
1/2 tsp. salt
1/2 tsp. garlic powder
3 large potatoes, peeled and cut into 1/2-inch thick lengthwise strips
1 medium green pepper, cut in rings

In medium skillet, melt butter. Add onion and red pepper and cook until
vegetables are tender. Stir in Parmesan cheese, salt and garlic powder.
Add peeled potato strips to skillet and toss to mix well. Turn into greased
1-quart baking dish. Arrange pepper rings on top. Bake covered at 350°
for 30 to 40 minutes or until potatoes are tender when pierced with a fork.
Yield: 4 to 6 servings.

▲ ▲ ▲

Whipped potato casserole

8 to 10 medium potatoes, peeled
1/4 to 1/2 cup milk
1 (8-oz.) pkg. cream cheese, softened
1 (8-oz.) carton sour cream
1/2 cup butter or margarine, melted
1/4 cup chopped chives
1 clove garlic, minced
2 tsp. salt
Paprika

Cook potatoes in boiling water about 30 minutes, or until tender. Drain and mash with milk. Beat softened cream cheese with an electric mixer until smooth. Add potatoes and remaining ingredients except paprika. Beat just until combined. Spoon mixture into a lightly buttered 2-quart casserole. Sprinkle with paprika. Cover and refrigerate overnight, if desired. Remove from refrigerator 15 minutes before baking. Uncover and bake at 350° for 30 minutes or until thoroughly heated. Yield: 8 to 10 servings.

▲ ▲ ▲

Lemon rice

This recipe came from Ken Fields, who ran a Kroger seafood department for many years. He especially liked to serve it with salmon.

1/3 cup butter or margarine
1 cup chopped celery
1 small onion, chopped
1 to 2 cups sliced fresh mushrooms (optional)
1/4 tsp. dried thyme
1 1/2 tsp. salt
1/8 tsp. pepper
2 tsp. grated lemon peel
1/4 cup lemon juice
1 1/3 cups water
1 3/4 cups instant rice

Melt butter or margarine in skillet and saute celery, onion and mushrooms (if used) about 5 minutes. Add thyme, salt, pepper, lemon peel, lemon juice and water. Bring to a boil. Mix in rice and cover. Remove from heat and let stand 5 minutes. Serve immediately.
To use regular rice instead of instant, combine 1 1/2 cups water, 1/4 cup lemon juice and 1 cup rice. Bring to boil, turn heat to simmer, cover and cook 17 minutes. Remove from heat and add the sauteed celery mixture. Yield: 6 to 8 servings.

▲ ▲ ▲
Spinach casserole

Johanna Parkins, Morristown, makes this casserole using fresh spinach.

3 lbs. spinach leaves, cleaned
3 cups light basic white sauce (instructions below)
1/2 tsp. dry mustard
1/2 cup sauteed finely diced onion
7 to 8 oz. Monterey Jack cheese with hot peppers, grated
1 to 2 tsp. juice from pickled hot jalapeno slices (to taste — for hotter version, also add minced jalapeno pepper)
1/2 tsp. black pepper
1 1/2 cups seasoned stuffing mix or seasoned bread crumbs
Light margarine

Wilt cleaned spinach leaves (cook a minute or two in the water that clings to the leaves, until leaves are wilted). Drain well. Chop coarsely.

Prepare white sauce: Melt 6 Tbsp. butter or margarine over medium heat. Add 4 Tbsp. flour, stirring occasionally; cook until bubbly, about 3 minutes. Add 3 cups milk (2% or skim). Reduce heat to medium-low and simmer, stirring with a whisk, until the sauce is thickened and smooth. Reduce heat and simmer for 5 minutes to remove any taste of uncooked flour. Season to taste with salt, pepper and 1/2 tsp. dry mustard.

Cook diced onion briefly in microwave (to avoid fat). Add to white sauce with grated cheese, jalapeno juice, black pepper and spinach. Pour into buttered casserole dish and top with stuffing mix or bread crumbs. Drizzle with margarine. Bake 20 to 30 minutes at 350° until bubbly.

▲ ▲ ▲
Spinach Maria

Spinach Maria, a dish served at Calhoun's, is one of our most requested recipes. From Marianne Birdwell of Knoxville comes this copy-cat version:

2 pkgs. frozen chopped spinach
1 medium onion, finely chopped
1 Tbsp. butter or margarine
1 (8-oz.) pkg. cream cheese
3/4 to 1 cup grated Parmesan cheese
1/2 to 3/4 tsp. ground cayenne pepper (use more or less, depending on how hot you like it)

Cook spinach according to package directions and drain on paper towels, squeezing out excess water. Saute onion in butter until tender. Add cream cheese and stir until melted. Add spinach, Parmesan cheese and cayenne pepper. Cook several minutes until well blended. Place in greased casserole dish and bake at 350° for 30 minutes. Yield: 4 servings.

▲ ▲ ▲

Rice-stuffed zucchini

Betty Lail, Seagrove, N.C., shares a recipe for rice-stuffed zucchini.

1 (7 or 8-oz.) pkg. chicken flavored Rice-a-Roni
Salt
4 medium zucchini
1 small tomato, chopped
1/2 cup shredded Muenster or Monterey Jack cheese

Prepare rice mix as directed on package.
Meanwhile, in large saucepan, bring 6 cups of water and 1 1/2 teaspoons salt to boil. Cut zucchini in half lengthwise. Add to boiling water and cook over medium heat 5 to 7 minutes, until zucchini is just tender-crisp. Immediately drain and cool under cold water for a few seconds.
Preheat oven to 375°. Using tip of teaspoon, scoop seeds out of zucchini, leaving shells 1/4- to 1/2-inch thick. In greased 9-by-13-inch dish, arrange zucchini crosswise. Sprinkle lightly with salt. Fill zucchini halves with rice. Top with chopped tomato and shredded cheese. Bake 10 minutes. Yield: 4 servings.

▲ ▲ ▲

Squash casserole

Amy McRary, News-Sentinel staff writer, offers a favorite squash recipe from her mother, Euna McRary, Granite Falls, N.C.

1 stick butter, melted
1 can cream of mushroom soup
1 (8-oz.) carton sour cream
2 to 3 cups cooked, chopped yellow squash (well-drained)
1 small chopped onion
3/4 of a small pkg. herb stuffing

Combine ingredients in 1-quart casserole. Bake at 350° for 20 minutes. Yield: 4 to 6 servings.

▲ ▲ ▲
* Light sweet potato souffle

1 (23-oz.) can sweet potatoes, mashed
1 Tbsp. soft diet margarine
1/3 cup hot skim milk
2 tsp. grated lemon rind
1/2 tsp. salt
Pepper, as desired
2 egg whites, stiffly beaten

Add hot milk and margarine to sweet potatoes and beat until fluffy. Add lemon rind, salt and pepper. Fold in stiffly beaten egg whites. Bake in greased casserole at 400° for 35 minutes. Yield: 4 servings.

▲ ▲ ▲
Sweet potato casserole

Novella Sharits of Knoxville offers this sweet potato casserole that she likes to serve at Thanksgiving.

3 cups mashed sweet potatoes (fresh cooked or canned)
1 cup granulated sugar
2 eggs
1/2 stick margarine
1/2 cup milk
1 Tbsp. vanilla
1/2 tsp. salt

Topping:
1 cup brown sugar
1/3 cup all-purpose flour
1/2 stick margarine, melted
1 cup chopped pecans (or other nuts)

If using fresh sweet potatoes, use 3 large or 5 medium potatoes for 3 cups mashed potatoes. Or use a 23-ounce can. Cook fresh potatoes by dropping them, unpeeled, in boiling water to cover and cook, covered, until tender, 25 to 30 minutes. Remove from water and cool slightly. Peel.
Mash either the fresh or canned potatoes (drained) with hand or electric beater, adding a little hot milk (about 1/4 cup) to make a smooth mixture. Add remaining ingredients and beat well. Pour into greased casserole and bake 30 minutes at 350°. Remove from oven. Add topping.
For topping: Combine brown sugar and flour. Add melted margarine and nuts. Spread over potatoes and return casserole to oven for 10 minutes at 350°. Yield: 6 servings.

▲ ▲ ▲

Falafel Hut tabbouleh

Renee Jubran of the Falafel Hut restaurant in Knoxville shares a tabbouleh recipe that her mother got from her mother. She says it's an authentic, ancient recipe.

1 cup bulgur (cracked wheat)	5 lemons
5 bunches fresh parsley	1/2 cup olive oil
6 medium ripe, firm tomatoes	1 tsp. salt
2 bunches green onions	1/2 tsp. ground black pepper
1 medium yellow onion	Dash allspice
1 bunch fresh mint (or 1 Tbsp. dried)	

Rinse the bulgur in cold water. Drain off all the excess water. (Bulgur is already cooked so it needs only rinsing and perhaps soaking to prepare.)

Remove stems from the parsley and discard. Chop the parsley very fine with a food processor and add to the bulgur. Dice tomatoes by hand and add to the bulgur. Dice the yellow onion and slice the green onions thinly, including the green tops. Add to the bulgur. Finely chop the mint and add to the bulgur. Mix these ingredients gently, using your hands.

Squeeze the lemons and add the juice to the bulgur mixture. Then add the oil, salt, pepper and allspice. Mix again by hand. Let the tabbouleh set for about 15 minutes before serving it so the dressing can be absorbed.

▲ ▲ ▲

Cooked turnips

Mary Comer, Dandridge, shares a recipe that comes from her mother, the late Mrs. Adrian Blanc, Jefferson City. The sauce is thin since it has no thickening added to it.

6 medium turnips, cleaned and peeled
Salt, pepper to taste
1/2 stick butter or margarine
1/2 cup sugar
Whole milk

Let whole turnips stand in cold water an hour or two — this is optional. Drain. Cook in pressure cooker, according to manufacturer's directions, for 10 minutes or until tender. (Turnips may be cooked in water in regular saucepan, covered, but it will take much longer.) Drain water. Add salt and pepper to taste. Add butter or margarine and sugar. Nearly cover whole turnips with milk. Cook on top of stove 20 minutes very fast to reduce sauce. Milk may curdle some, but the sauce tastes great. Alternately, the turnips with milk could be poured into a casserole and baked at 350° for 30 to 40 minutes. Yield: 6 servings.

Main dishes

▲ ▲ ▲
Main dishes

▲ ▲ ▲
Buster Keaton casserole

Attorney Sharon Lee of Madisonville sends "the original" Buster Keaton casserole recipe. A reader liked the dish when it was served at the Cat's Meow Restaurant that was formerly on Cumberland Avenue in Knoxville.

1 1/2 lbs. ground beef
24 oz. tomato sauce
Garlic powder
Seasoned salt
8 oz. cream cheese, softened
1/4 cup sour cream
1 (8-oz.) carton cottage cheese
1/2 cup chopped onion
1 (8-oz.) pkg. medium noodles

Brown ground beef; drain. Add tomato sauce. Season with garlic powder and seasoned salt (to taste). Simmer 10 to 15 minutes. Combine softened cream cheese, sour cream, cottage cheese and onion. Cook noodles according to package directions and drain.

Grease a 13-by-9-by-2-inch casserole and layer in half the noodles. Top with cheese mixture, then remaining noodles. Top with meat sauce. Bake at 375° for 45 minutes. Yield: 10 to 12 servings.

Casserole freezes well. It also may be prepared ahead, refrigerated and baked at serving time.

▲ ▲ ▲
Mexican casserole

Clarice Harris offers an easy-to-make dish. Leftovers freeze well for another meal.

10 oz. ground beef or ground turkey
1 medium onion, chopped
1 cup water
1 (16-oz.) can pinto beans
1 pkg. taco mix
2 cups tomato sauce
9 small flour tortillas
6 oz. cheddar cheese, shredded

Brown meat and onions. Add water, pinto beans and taco mix. Bring to boil, turn heat down and simmer. Dip 6 tortillas into tomato sauce and then line 9-by-13-inch pan with the tortillas. Pour ground meat mixture over the tortillas. Top with last three tortillas. Top with remaining tomato sauce and cheddar cheese. Bake at 350° for 30 minutes. Yield: 8 to 10 servings.

▲ ▲ ▲

Mexican cheese casserole

Carrie Johnson, Maryville, sends a Mexican cheese casserole recipe that came from California.

1 lb. ground beef, browned and drained
2 cans cream of mushroom soup
1 small can green chilies, chopped
1/4 cup chopped onion
1/2 lb. Monterey Jack cheese, grated
1/2 lb. cheddar cheese, grated
10 to 12 flour tortillas

Brown meat and drain off fat. In a large bowl combine soup, chilies and onion. Add meat. Add half of each cheese. Mix. Put about 2 tablespoons of the mixture on each tortilla and roll up tortilla. Place rolls in large baking dish, putting them close together. If any mixture remains, spread it over rolls. Sprinkle rolls with the other half of each cheese. Bake 15 to 30 minutes at 350° until cheese melts and rolls are hot through.

▲ ▲ ▲

Quick pizza casserole

Mary Jones, Jefferson City, sends a casserole recipe that is quick and easy.

1 1/2 lb. ground beef
1 (14-oz.) jar pizza sauce
2 cups (8-oz.) shredded mozzarella cheese
3/4 cup Bisquick
1 1/2 cups milk
2 eggs

Brown meat over medium heat, stirring to crumble. Drain. Spoon meat into an 8-inch baking dish. Top with pizza sauce and cheese. Combine Bisquick, milk and eggs, beating until smooth. Pour mixture over beef, sauce and cheese, covering evenly. Bake at 400° for 30 to 35 minutes.
    Yield: 6 servings.

▲ ▲ ▲

Oriental beef-spaghetti casserole

Phyllis Rainwater of Dandridge makes a casserole with a catchy name. It may be baked and served or made and frozen.

1 (7-oz.) package thin spaghetti, broken up
1 Tbsp. vegetable oil
1/2 lb. ground beef
1/2 lb. ground pork (or omit pork and use 1 1/2 pounds ground chuck)
1/3 cup chopped onion
1 cup chopped celery
1/2 cup chopped green pepper
1 (6-oz.) can tomato paste
1 cup lemon-lime carbonated beverage
1/2 cup ketchup
1/4 tsp. thyme
1 (4-oz.) can sliced mushrooms
1 (1-lb.) can chop suey vegetables, drained
1 1/2 tsp. salt (or to taste)
3/4 cup grated Parmesan cheese
1/2 to 3/4 cup buttered bread crumbs (optional)

Cook spaghetti according to package directions; drain and set aside. Heat vegetable oil in large skillet or pan. Add beef, pork, onion, celery and green pepper. Cook for 10 minutes on medium heat, stirring occasionally to brown the beef. Drain well on paper towels and pour off any grease that has formed.

Return meat and vegetables to pan. Add tomato paste, lemon-lime carbonated beverage, ketchup, thyme, mushrooms, chop suey vegetables and salt. Simmer 10 minutes. Add more lemon-lime carbonated beverage if mixture becomes too thick.

In two casseroles, each about 6-by-10 inches, place a layer of cooked spaghetti and a layer of meat sauce. Sprinkle with Parmesan cheese and buttered bread crumbs.

Bake at 350° about 30 minutes, until hot and bubbly. Each casserole serves 4 to 6.

To freeze: After casserole is prepared, let cool completely.

Cover tightly with foil and seal. To serve, thaw and bake.

▲ ▲ ▲

* Stroganoff casserole

Chris Bryant, Johnson City, sends a recipe for a casserole that may be prepared ahead, refrigerated and baked at serving time. It also freezes well.

1 1/2 lbs. ground chuck
24 oz. tomato sauce
Garlic powder
1 (8-oz.) pkg. light cream cheese, softened
1/4 cup light sour cream
8 oz. low-fat cottage cheese
1/2 cup chopped onion
1 (8-oz.) pkg. medium noodles

Brown meat and drain well. Return to skillet and add tomato sauce. Season with garlic powder to taste. Simmer 10 to 15 minutes.

Combine softened cream cheese, sour cream, cottage cheese and onion. Cook noodles according to package directions and drain.

Lightly grease casserole. Layer half the noodles on the bottom; top with cream cheese mixture, then remaining noodles. Top with meat sauce. Bake at 375° for 45 minutes. Yield: 8 servings.

▲ ▲ ▲

Cheeseburger pie

When a reader requested the recipe for cheeseburger pie, Sarajune Owen of Townsend, Marni Shirley of Caryville, Ann Pearch of Harriman, Wanda Davis of Sevierville, Dorothy Jinks of Morristown and Gerry Troy of Knoxville replied.

1 cup Bisquick mix	2 Tbsp. Bisquick mix
1/4 cup cold water	1 Tbsp. Worcestershire sauce
1 lb. ground beef	2 eggs
1/2 cup chopped onion	1 cup small curd cottage cheese
1/2 tsp. salt	2 medium tomatoes, sliced
1/4 tsp. pepper	1 cup shredded cheddar cheese

Heat oven to 375°. Mix Bisquick and water until soft dough forms. Beat vigorously 20 strokes. Gently smooth dough into ball on floured cloth-covered board. Knead 5 times. Roll dough 2 inches larger than inverted pie plate, 9-by-1 1/4-inches. Ease dough into plate; flute edge, if desired.

Cook and stir ground beef and onion until beef is brown; drain. Stir in salt, pepper, 2 tablespoons Bisquick and the Worcestershire sauce. Spoon into pie crust. Mix eggs and cottage cheese. Pour over beef mixture. Arrange tomato slices in circle on top. Sprinkle with cheddar cheese. Bake until set, about 30 minutes. Yield: 6 to 8 servings.

▲ ▲ ▲

Chef Ludwig's pepper steak

This recipe came from the Hyatt Regency, Atlanta, at its opening in the mid-1970s. It's been one of our family favorites since.

3 tsp. butter or margarine
1 small sweet green pepper
1/2 medium red pepper (or pimento)
1/4 medium onion
1 medium ripe tomato
1 tsp. vegetable oil
1 (12-oz.) sirloin steak
1 Tbsp. cracked black pepper

Put butter or margarine in saucepan and let melt. Thinly slice the peppers, onion and tomato. Add to butter in saucepan, stir-frying until tender. Pour vegetable oil into skillet and heat until it is very hot. Press cracked black pepper into steak. Brown steak on each side in hot skillet. Pour vegetables over top. Place in 400° oven and cook until steak is of desired doneness. Serve immediately. Yield: 2 to 4 servings.

▲ ▲ ▲

Lasagna

News-Sentinel staff writer Amy McRary gave us a lasagna recipe that has become our favorite. When you make it, make only two layers. The casserole overflows with three layers, so if necessary, make a small casserole, too.

1 lb. ground beef and/or sausage
1 clove garlic, minced
1 onion, chopped
3 Tbsp. fresh parsley
1 Tbsp. fresh basil
2 tsp. salt
2 cups canned tomatoes
1 (12-oz.) can tomato paste
3 cups cottage cheese
2 beaten eggs
1/2 tsp. pepper
1/2 cup grated Parmesan cheese
1 lb. thinly sliced mozzarella
8 oz. lasagna noodles, cooked

Brown meat and drain well on paper towels. Add onion and garlic, cooking until tender. In large pan, combine, meat, onion, garlic, 1 tablespoon of parsley, basil, 1 teaspoon salt, tomatoes and tomato paste. Simmer uncovered until thick, about 30 minutes, stirring occasionally.

Combine in a bowl the cottage cheese, eggs, 1 teaspoon salt, pepper, 2 tablespoons parsley and grated Parmesan cheese.

Place half of the cooked lasagna noodles in greased 13-by-9-by-2-inch baking dish. Cover with half the mozzarella cheese, half the cottage cheese filling, then half the meat sauce. Repeat layers.

Bake at 375° for 30 minutes. Let stand 10 to 15 minutes before cutting in squares to serve. Yield: 6 to 8 servings.

▲ ▲ ▲

Lasagna roll-ups

Anne Christophory, Jefferson City, makes lasagna roll-ups. The design of the rolls is almost star-shaped when they're cut, so the dish is attractive enough to set on the table and serve.

6 uncooked lasagna noodles
6 uncooked spinach (or plain) lasagna noodles
1 lb. Italian sausage links
2 lbs. ground beef
2 large onions, chopped (about 2 cups)
2 jars (15 1/2-oz. each) spaghetti sauce or 3 cups homemade
1 can (8-oz.) mushroom stems and pieces, undrained
3 cups ricotta or creamed cottage cheese
1 (10-oz.) pkg. frozen chopped spinach, thawed and well drained
1/2 cup grated Parmesan cheese
1 tsp. salt
1/4 tsp. pepper
2 cloves garlic, crushed
1 egg, well beaten

Cook noodles as directed on package; drain. Cover noodles with cold water. Squeeze meat out of Italian sausage links and cook with the beef and onion in 10-inch skillet until beef is brown. Drain well. Stir in spaghetti sauce and mushrooms. Heat to boiling. Pour sauce into ungreased rectangular baking dish.

Because of the amount of sauce, a deep dish or pan is needed, such as a turkey roaster pan. Combine ricotta or cottage cheese, well-drained spinach, Parmesan cheese, salt, pepper, crushed garlic cloves and egg.

Drain cold water off the noodles. Place noodles out flat on a surface and spread 3 heaping tablespoons of the cheese mixture to the edges of each noodle. Roll each noodle up and cut each roll in half. Place rolls, cut sides down, in beef sauce in the dish or pan. Bake in 350° oven until hot and bubbly, about 40 minutes.

If dish is not covered during baking, the sauce becomes thick. If you prefer a thin sauce, cover the casserole.

Yield: 8 servings, 3 roll-ups per person.

▲ ▲ ▲

Mother-in-law's meat loaf

Janet Musick of Knoxville writes: "When I was still a newlywed, my mother-in-law gave me this recipe, advising me it was the only meat loaf her son would eat. She was right!"

1 1/2 lbs. ground beef
2 cups fresh bread crumbs
1 medium onion, chopped
1 1/2 tsp. salt
1/4 tsp. pepper
4 oz. tomato sauce
1 egg, beaten
Sweet-sour sauce (recipe follows) or a barbecue sauce

Lightly mix all ingredients except sweet-sour sauce. Form into a loaf. Bake in shallow pan at 350°. While it's beginning to bake, combine the following for sauce:

Sweet-sour sauce:
4 oz. tomato sauce
2 Tbsp. prepared mustard
2 Tbsp. brown sugar or molasses
2 Tbsp. vinegar
1/2 cup water

Combine ingredients and pour over meat loaf. Continue to bake 1 1/2 hours longer, basting meat with sauce occasionally.
Note: Between 2 tsp. and 2 Tbsp. dry mustard may be used instead of prepared mustard, according to taste.

▲ ▲ ▲

Juicy meat loaf

Betty Reams, Morristown, shares her aunt's meat loaf recipe.

1 1/2 lbs. ground beef
3/4 cup oats
2 eggs, beaten
1/4 cup chopped onions
1/4 cup chopped green pepper

1/4 tsp. pepper
1 cup tomato juice
1 can cream of celery soup
1 cup corn bread crumbs
Salt
Sweet-sour sauce (see above)

Mix all together except sauce and form into one large or two small loaves. Pour sauce over loaves. Bake at 350° for 1 hour basting occasionally with sauce. Yield: 4 servings.

▲ ▲ ▲

Reuben meat loaf

Nancy Boatman, Rockford, sends this different version of meat loaf. She says cheddar cheese may be used instead of Swiss. She leaves out the pastrami for "picky eaters" in the family.

2 lbs. ground beef
2 cups soft bread crumbs
1 egg, slightly beaten
2 Tbsp. ketchup
3/4 tsp. salt
1 (8-oz.) can sauerkraut, rinsed and drained
1 cup shredded Swiss cheese
1/4 lb. pastrami, chopped
1/4 cup dairy sour cream
1 Tbsp. prepared yellow mustard

Combine ground beef, bread crumbs, egg, ketchup and salt in a bowl, mixing lightly. Combine sauerkraut, 3/4 cup of the Swiss cheese, pastrami, sour cream and mustard. Pat out a third of meat mixture to form an oval 9-inches long on an oven proof platter or baking dish. Spread half of sauerkraut mixture over meat. Repeat layers of meat and kraut mixtures, using a third of meat mixture for top layer of loaf.

Bake at 350° for 1 hour, loosely covered with foil. Remove foil. Sprinkle remaining cheese on top and bake 5 more minutes. Yield: 6 to 8 servings.

▲ ▲ ▲

Shepherd's pie

When a reader wanted a recipe for shepherd's pie from Historic Rugby, Mary Alice Cox of Clinton sent it.

1/2 cup chopped onions
1 cup thinly sliced carrots
1 stick butter
2 cups chopped leftover roast beef
1 cup gravy made from beef drippings
1 beef bouillon cube
4 tsp. parsley
2 bay leaves
Dash of sage
Salt, pepper to taste
4 cups mashed potatoes
1/2 cup grated sharp cheddar

Saute onion and carrot in butter, just until tender. Combine with the roast beef, gravy, bouillon cube and seasonings. Simmer for 10 minutes.

If the consistency is thin or soupy, add a little flour to thicken. Remove bay leaves. Put the mixture into four individual casserole dishes. Top with mashed potatoes and spread smooth. Mark top of potato with tines of a fork. Sprinkle with grated cheese. Bake at 375° until hot and cheese is golden and bubbly. Garnish with fresh parsley, if desired.

▲ ▲ ▲

Baked spaghetti

Glenda Burnett of Knoxville says this spaghetti recipe from Recipes and Requests is one of her favorites.

1 medium onion, chopped
1 medium green pepper, chopped
1 clove garlic, minced
1 lb. ground beef
2 cans Franco-American spaghetti with cheese
3/4 (5-oz.) jar Old English cheese
1 (2-oz.) can mushroom pieces, drained

Stir fry onion, pepper and garlic in small amount of oil. Add ground beef and cook until the beef is browned. Drain well. Add spaghetti with cheese, Old English cheese and mushrooms. Pour in casserole dish, covered or uncovered. If uncovered, stir occasionally. Bake at 350° for 40 minutes. Top with Parmesan cheese, if desired. Yield: 4 servings.

▲ ▲ ▲

Savory baked spaghetti

Wanda Davis of Sevierville shares a quick and easy recipe that uses uncooked spaghetti.

2 medium onions, coarsely chopped
3 Tbsp. bacon grease or vegetable oil
1 clove garlic (optional)
1/2 lb. ground chuck
1/2 tsp. salt
1/8 tsp. pepper
1 (1-lb. 13-oz.) can tomatoes (3 1/2 cups)
1 tsp. chili powder
1 cup water
1 (8-oz.) pkg. spaghetti, uncooked
1/4 lb. cheddar cheese, grated (1 cup)

Cook onions and garlic in bacon grease or oil in skillet for 5 minutes.
Add chuck; cook, stirring occasionally, until meat loses its red color. Stir in salt, pepper and tomatoes. Simmer, covered, 30 minutes. Discard garlic. Add chili powder and water.
Break half of uncooked spaghetti into greased 2-quart casserole. Pour on half of sauce. Sprinkle with half of cheese. Repeat layers.
Bake covered 35 minutes at 325°. Uncover and bake 15 minutes longer or until brown. Yield: 6 servings.

▲ ▲ ▲

Italian spaghetti for a crowd

Ruth Sutton, who was hostess at the former Miller's Laurel Room in Knoxville, gave us a recipe for Italian spaghetti for a crowd. She says in the late 1950s Chef Trammel at Rich's (which the Henley Street department store was before it became Miller's, then Hess's) made "unbelievably delicious" spaghetti.

4 lbs. ground beef or 3 lbs. beef and 1 lb. ground pork
4 large onions, chopped fine
2 cloves garlic, chopped fine
3 (15-oz.) cans tomatoes
3 (8-oz.) cans tomato sauce
1/4 cup olive oil
2 Tbsp. sugar
1 Tbsp. salt or to taste
1 Tbsp. basil
1 Tbsp. oregano
1 Tbsp. dry mustard
2 Tbsp. parsley flakes
1 tsp. Tabasco sauce
2 (16-oz.) pkgs. spaghetti
Grated cheese

Place ground meat in large skillet and brown. Drain off grease. Add all ingredients except the spaghetti and cheese. Simmer 2 or more hours.

Cook spaghetti according to package directions and drain. Serve with the sauce. Sprinkle with grated American or Parmesan cheese, if desired. Yield: 16 to 18 servings.

▲ ▲ ▲
Stuffed green peppers

Ada Julian of Knoxville shares a recipe for stuffed peppers that she likes especially well. They may be cooked in a slow cooker. If frozen, set in refrigerator overnight and put in slow cooker while still icy. Add the sauce to the slow cooker.

4 green peppers (8 halves)
1 lb. ground beef, browned
1 onion, chopped
1 cup softened bread crumbs
1 egg
2 Tbsp. ketchup
Salt, pepper to taste
1 Tbsp. chopped green pepper

Sauce:
1/2 cup ketchup
1/4 cup water
Dash Worchestershire sauce
Dash Heinz 57 meat sauce

Thickening:
2 Tbsp. flour
1/2 cup water
1/2 tsp. Kitchen Bouquet

Wash peppers, cut in halves, remove seeds and membrane. Pre-cook in boiling salted water about 3 minutes. Drain well. Mix meat, onion, salt, pepper, bread crumbs, egg, ketchup. Stuff into pepper halves. Place in baking dish.

Combine sauce ingredients. Pour over the peppers. Cover with lid or foil and bake 20 minutes at 350°. Remove cover and bake 5 more minutes.

Meanwhile combine flour, water and Kitchen Bouquet, stirring until smooth. Remove peppers from dish and add thickening to sauce in the baking dish. Bring to a boil to thicken sauce. Serve sauce over peppers. Yield: 4 servings.

▲ ▲ ▲

Easy tamales

White Lily Foods Co. offers an easy recipe for making tamales, which is even easier if you have friends in the kitchen to help with the steps involved. Step one is deciding whether to use corn husks or tamale papers to wrap. (Usually tamale papers are found at meat departments and corn husks in the produce section of a supermarket. If not in view, ask.)
It takes about 15 minutes longer to boil or steam tamales in corn husks than in papers. It is also easier to work with the tamale papers because they are more pliable and uniformly-shaped. With corn husks, strings need to be tied around both directions of the envelope-shaped package, and corn husks must soak 30 minutes before they are pliable enough to work with. If refrigerating or freezing tamales, however, the corn husks seem to keep the cornmeal mixture more moist.
Tamales freeze well. They may be completely prepared a day ahead and refrigerated. When ready to serve, microwave (about six minutes to reheat six tamales). They may be partially prepared – wrapped in papers, but not boiled, and refrigerated. At serving time, complete the cooking, about an hour.
Use exact measurements when making the tamales – three tablespoons of dough and two tablespoons of filling – to make the dough and filling come out evenly.

Filling:
1 lb. ground beef
1 medium onion, chopped
1/4 cup self-rising cornmeal mix
2 Tbsp. chili powder
1/2 tsp. salt
1/4 tsp. pepper
1/4 tsp. garlic powder

Tamales:
4 cups self-rising cornmeal mix
2/3 cup vegetable shortening
1 1/2 tsp. salt
1 1/2 tsp. chili powder
1 1/2 to 2 cups boiling water
Tamale papers or corn husks
String
Chili

Filling: Brown ground beef and onion over medium heat. Remove from heat and stir in cornmeal mix, chili powder, salt, pepper and garlic powder.

Tamales: Combine cornmeal mix, shortening, salt and chili powder. Blend well. Stir in just enough boiling water to make a soft dough. (Start with 1 1/2 cups, then add more while using the cornmeal mixture. The trick in making tamales is keeping the dough moist.)

Soak tamale papers or corn husks in warm water until soft. Take a paper or corn husk out and flatten it on a clean counter or cutting board. Spread paper or husk with approximately 3 tablespoons tamale mixture, making a rectangle 3 1/2-by-4 1/2-inches.

Place 2 tablespoons meat mixture lengthwise down center of rectangle. Roll up bottom edge of tamale paper so tamale mixture wraps completely around meat filling. Continue rolling, tucking both sides of paper in to produce a smooth, sealed roll. Tie tamales securely with string.

Carefully place tamales, seam side down, in boiling water (or in a steamer set in boiling water). Boil covered 45 minutes. Drain. To serve: Spoon prepared chili over unwrapped tamales. Makes 1 1/2 to 2 dozen.

▲ ▲ ▲

Hot tamales

Mrs. Clyde Yarber, Clinton, offers this recipe.

2 lbs. cornmeal
1 cup flour
1 1/2 tsp. salt
1/2 cup shortening
Boiling water
1 lb. hamburger, browned
1 lb. sausage, browned
1 tsp. salt
1 large can Mexican chili powder
1/2 tsp. pepper
Tamale papers

Mix cornmeal, flour, salt and shortening with enough boiling water to make mixture stick together. Place a small amount of batter, enough for 1 tamale, on lightly floured board or waxed paper. Pat thin. Spread with mixture of cooked meat, salt, chili powder and pepper and roll. Place in tamale paper and tie each end with strong twine. When all the tamales are wrapped, place in kettle of boiling water. Boil covered for 2 hours. Turn off heat and let simmer 15 to 20 minutes.

Makes 12 to 16 tamales. Cool and place in plastic bags to freeze. To use after freezing, drop frozen into boiling water for 20 minutes.

▲ ▲ ▲

Walk-around

Chili spooned into a package of corn chips is a delicious supper the youngsters will enjoy helping to prepare. The treats were popular at Knoxville's World Fair.

1 (individual size) pkg. corn chips   **Chopped lettuce (optional)**
Chili   **Chopped onion**
Grated American or cheddar cheese   **Taco sauce (hot or mild)**
Chopped tomato   **Sour cream**

Take a bag of corn chips, turn it sideways and carefully trim off the edge of the bag to form a length-wise pouch. Hold it in a paper napkin or towel. Ladle hot chili onto chips. Place remaining ingredients on chili and top with sour cream. Eat out of the bag with a spoon.

Note: To layer in a casserole, place corn chips on bottom; top with chopped onion, grated cheese, chili, more corn chips and more cheese. Bake at 350° until hot and bubbly. Some people prefer not to bake the casserole, but to let the hot chili melt the cheese. This leaves the corn chips very crisp.

▲ ▲ ▲

Ham loaf

Shirley Hileman of Knoxville makes a ham loaf that is excellent for entertaining.

2 lbs. ground uncooked ham
1 lb. hamburger
2 cups milk
3 eggs
2 cups cornflake crumbs

Basting ingredients:
1/2 cup brown sugar
1/2 cup vinegar

Mix all ingredients (except basting ingredients). Form into 12 to 15 individual loaves or 1 big one. Place on 9-by-13-inch pan. Bake at 350° for 30 minutes for small loaves; 90 minutes for large loaf. Pour basting mixture over meat. Bake 15 minutes more, basting once again. Yield: 12 servings.

▲ ▲ ▲

Ham sandwiches

Phyllis Rainwater of Dandridge freezes ham sandwiches that are similar to those you might buy at Arby's.

1/2 lb. butter or margarine
3 Tbsp. (or less) poppy seeds
1 tsp. Worcestershire sauce
3 Tbsp. mustard-horseradish sauce
1 medium onion, grated
1 lb. grated Swiss cheese
1/2 lb. grated American cheese
5 packages wafer-thin chipped ham
2 pkgs. (8-each) hamburger buns with sesame seeds

Mix butter, seeds, sauce, mustard-horseradish and grated onion. Spread thickly on both sides of buns. Using scissors, cut ham to fit buns and place on bottom half of buns. Cover with cheese and place top half on. (Sandwiches will be very thick.) Wrap in foil and freeze individually.

Remove from freezer and let thaw a little. Unwrap foil and warm sandwiches, still on the foil, about 20 minutes at 350°, until cheese melts. Yield: 16 sandwiches.

▲ ▲ ▲
Pork barbecue

A pork barbecue recipe comes from a Knoxville reader who got it from a neighbor in Atlanta who was from New York! Jennie Newcomb writes that the barbecue is different from the recipes she has seen in the South. She usually buys a pork loin and has it sliced 1 1/2-inches thick. She then trims off as much fat as possible and cooks the pork in the sauce a day before serving. When the meat is refrigerated, the fat comes to the top so she can take off the rest of it.

Pork tenderloin
1 onion
Juice of 1 lemon
1/2 tsp. dry mustard
1 Tbsp. brown sugar

1/2 cup ketchup
1/2 cup water
1 tsp. salt
1/4 cup Worcestershire sauce

Brown sliced pork in 450° oven about 30 minutes. Combine remaining ingredients in saucepan, doubling or tripling amounts if necessary. Simmer 10 minutes. Pour over meat. Cover and bake 1 1/2 hours at 325°. Uncover and brown 15 minutes.

Note: It is possible to cook the barbecue sauce and meat in a slow cooker after browning the meat under the broiler. Double or triple the sauce until there is enough to cover the amount of pork used.

▲ ▲ ▲
Sausage-rice casserole

Iona Delionback, Maryville, offers this casserole. It dates to the time she had World's Fair visitors and makes enough for three casserole dishes. It can be cut in third for one small casserole.

3 (1-lb.) pkgs. sausage (1 hot, 2 mild)
6 cups chopped celery
3 cups chopped onion
3 cups cooked rice
3 cups undiluted cream of chicken soup
1 cup chopped green peppers
2 cups chopped pecans
Stuffed olives, sliced

Brown sausage, pour off grease. Add celery and onions. Cook for 3 minutes. Add rice, soup and peppers. Simmer for 3 minutes. Pour into two or three casserole dishes and top with pecans. (Dish can be frozen at this point, if desired.)

Bake at 300° for 30 to 35 minutes (or longer if dish is frozen). Top with sliced olives just before serving. Yield: 12 servings.

▲ ▲ ▲

Sausage-spinach quiche

From White Lily Foods Co. comes a quiche that can be a main dish.

9-inch unbaked deep-dish pie shell
1 3/4 cups sliced fresh mushrooms
1 Tbsp. butter or margarine
1 (12-oz.) pkg. frozen spinach souffle, thawed
1/2 lb. hot sausage, cooked and crumbled
1 cup shredded Swiss cheese
2 eggs, beaten
3 Tbsp. milk
1/2 tsp. pepper
1/2 tsp. hot pepper sauce
1/4 tsp. nutmeg

Prepare pastry for 9-inch deep-dish pie pan or use a purchased deep-dish pie crust. Bake for 9 minutes at 450° or until lightly browned. In large skillet, lightly brown mushrooms in butter or margarine until tender. Drain well. Combine mushrooms, spinach souffle, sausage, cheese, eggs, milk, pepper, hot pepper sauce and nutmeg. Stir well. Pour into baked pie crust.

Wrap edge of crust with aluminum foil to prevent over browning. Bake at 350° for 35 to 40 minutes or until set. Let stand 10 minutes before serving. Yield: 6 servings.

▲ ▲ ▲

Chicken casserole

This is an easy-to-make casserole for company. It needs to be prepared a day ahead, including the crushed potato chips on top, and refrigerated overnight.

4 cups diced cooked chicken
  (about 6 breast halves, cooked)
2 cups finely chopped celery
4 hard-cooked eggs, chopped
1 tsp. chopped onion
1 large jar chopped pimentos, drained
1 (2-oz.) can mushrooms, drained

3/4 cup mayonnaise
1 can cream of chicken soup
2 Tbsp. lemon juice
2/3 cup sliced almonds
1 cup grated sharp cheese
1 1/2 cups crushed potato chips

Combine chicken, celery, chopped eggs, onion, pimentos and mushrooms in 9-by-13-inch baking dish. Combine mayonnaise, soup and lemon juice and stir into mixture. Sprinkle with sliced almonds, grated cheese and crushed potato chips. Refrigerate overnight. Bake at 400° for 25 to 30 minutes. Yield: 10 to 12 servings.

▲ ▲ ▲

Chicken and pasta

Dot McKenry of Knoxville shares a chicken casserole recipe that she often uses for cookouts and Big Orange tailgate activities.

3/4 cup mayonnaise
1/3 cup flour
2 Tbsp. instant minced onion
1 tsp. garlic salt
2 1/4 cups milk
1 cup shredded Swiss cheese
1/3 cup white wine
1 (7-oz.) pkg. spaghetti, cooked and drained
2 cups cooked chicken
1 (10-oz.) pkg. frozen chopped broccoli, thawed and drained
1 1/4 cups sliced natural almonds (untoasted with skins on)
1 (4-oz.) can sliced mushrooms, drained
1/4 cup chopped pimentos
Grated Parmesan cheese

In medium saucepan, combine mayonnaise, flour and seasonings. Gradually add milk and Swiss cheese. Cook over low heat, stirring constantly until cheese melts. Remove from heat and stir in wine. Combine mayonnaise mixture, spaghetti, chicken, broccoli, 3/4 cup almonds, mushrooms and pimentos. Toss lightly. Pour mixture into baking dish. Top with remaining almonds. Bake at 350° for 45 minutes. Serve with Parmesan cheese. Yield: 8 servings.

▲ ▲ ▲
Chicken pot pie

From Georgie Diane Lee, Harriman, comes this recipe.

1 stewing chicken
1 can cream of celery soup
1 (16-oz.) can mixed vegetables
1 cup chicken broth
Biscuit dough or canned biscuits

Biscuit dough:
4 cups self-rising flour
1 stick melted butter
2 Tbsp. mayonnaise
Milk

Cut chicken into pieces and place in a stewing pan with water to cover. Bring to a boil, reduce heat and simmer until chicken is tender, about 2 hours or more. Remove chicken; save broth. Let chicken cool and shred meat off the bones. Place chicken in bottom of 9-by-13-inch casserole. Combine celery soup, vegetables and 1 cup chicken broth and pour over chicken. Top with biscuit dough.

To make biscuits: Combine ingredients. Add milk to desired thickness. Pour over chicken mixture. Bake at 350° until biscuit top is brown, about 30 minutes.

Note: If using canned biscuits, place them on chicken mixture, bake about half the time, or until biscuits are brown on top. Turn biscuits over and bake again to brown other side. Yield: 8 to 10 servings.

▲ ▲ ▲
Chicken rotel

Sherri Gardner-Howell, News-Sentinel columnist, shares this recipe.

1 fryer or stewing chicken
1 cup chopped onion
1 cup chopped bell peppers
1 cup chopped celery
Butter or margarine

1 (12-oz.) pkg. wide egg noodles
1 (10-oz.) can Rotel tomatoes
  and green chilies
1 lb. Velveeta cheese
1 pkg. Ritz crackers

Stew chicken in about 3 cups water until tender. Remove chicken, cool, debone and cut in bite-size pieces. Strain and save broth.

Stir-fry onions, peppers and celery in butter until tender. Cook noodles in chicken broth until tender. (Add water to broth if necessary to make enough liquid for cooking noodles.) Drain noodles and mix with chicken, onion mixture, tomatoes and cheese cut into cubes in a very large casserole or two small casseroles. (Freeze one casserole, if desired.) Crumble crackers and sprinkle over the top. Cook at 300° about 15 to 20 minutes or until hot. Yield: 10 to 12 servings.

▲ ▲ ▲

Creamed chicken or turkey

Jewel Thomas, Lenoir City, says this recipe for creamed chicken or turkey in a corn bread ring sounds complicated, but it really isn't.

3 Tbsp. butter or margarine
4 Tbsp. flour
1 cup chicken stock
1 cup whole milk
3/4 to 1 1/2 cups diced cooked chicken or turkey
1/8 tsp. pepper
3/4 tsp. salt
1 tsp. minced onion
1/2 tsp. paprika

Prepare sauce as follows: Melt margarine; add flour and stir over low heat until blended. Slowly add chicken stock and milk, stirring to mix well. Stir and cook until thickened. Then set over hot water in top of double boiler or over low heat. Add chicken and seasonings. Heat thoroughly. Serve very hot.

Corn bread ring:
1 cup flour
1 cup cornmeal
2 Tbsp. sugar
4 tsp. baking powder
1/2 tsp. salt
1 tsp. poultry seasoning
1/2 tsp. sage
1 cup milk
1 egg
1/4 cup vegetable oil, corn oil or melted butter

Sift dry ingredients together into medium-size bowl. Add the egg, milk and oil. Do not overbeat. Pour into a greased 8-inch ring mold and bake at 425° for 20 to 25 minutes. Turn onto platter. Fill center with creamed chicken or turkey. Yield: 8 servings.

▲ ▲ ▲
Curry chicken

Nita Noe of Knoxville contributes a recipe for curry chicken that is a great way to use leftover chicken or turkey.

4 cups cooked chicken or turkey
3 cans chicken broth or 3 pints homemade chicken broth
2 cans cream of chicken soup
1 1/2 tsp. curry powder
Salt, pepper to taste
1 stick margarine
3 Tbsp. cornstarch
1 1/2 cups white wine
Cooked noodles or rice

Combine chicken, broth, soup, curry powder, salt, pepper and margarine. Bring almost to boiling, turn heat down and simmer 30 minutes or longer. Dissolve cornstarch in white wine and stir into chicken mixture, stirring until mixture thickens. Serve over noodles or rice. Yield: 8 servings.

▲ ▲ ▲
* Turkey chili

Turkey chili is a healthy alternative to ground beef chili. Terry Ahrens, Food City director of consumer affairs in Abingdon, Va., says tasters won't even know this chili is made with ground turkey instead of beef. It seems like a lot of seasonings, but it turns out fine. If you want it hotter, add more chili powder or cayenne pepper.

2 lbs. raw ground turkey
2 Tbsp. margarine
1/2 cup chopped onion
2 garlic cloves, minced
2 Tbsp. chili powder, or more to taste
2 tsp. ground cumin
1 Tbsp. paprika
1 (28-oz.) can tomatoes
1 (15-oz.) can red kidney beans
1 (15-oz.) can pinto beans
1 tsp. salt
Freshly ground pepper to taste

Cook turkey and onions in margarine until turkey is no longer pink. Add garlic, chili powder, cumin, paprika, tomatoes, beans, salt and pepper. Cover. Bring to a boil over high heat, then reduce heat and simmer 45 minutes to an hour to cook some of the liquid down.

Chili is best when prepared a day ahead, refrigerated and simmered an hour just before serving. Yield: 8 servings.

Note: Serve topped with grated cheddar cheese, if desired.

▲ ▲ ▲

Turkey meat loaf

Mrs. I.V. Goins sends a turkey meat loaf recipe that is a favorite where she works. She cooks it for children, ages 1 to 6, at a day care center.

2 lbs. raw ground turkey
2 eggs
2 cups packaged bread stuffing mix
1 can tomato soup
3 Tbsp. Worcestershire sauce
1 tsp. sage

Combine ingredients. Shape into loaf and place in large baking dish. Bake at 350° for 1 hour to 1 hour, 15 minutes. Yield: 6 to 8 servings.

▲ ▲ ▲

* Turkey meat loaves

Joan Cohn of Knoxville sends this turkey meat loaf recipe. Turkey meat loaf is becoming popular with those who want healthy dishes.

1 onion, chopped
1 garlic clove, minced
2 Tbsp. olive oil
2 tomatoes, peeled,
   seeded and chopped
1/2 tsp. oregano
1/2 tsp. basil
1/4 cup dry red wine

1 large bell pepper, chopped
1 zucchini, chopped
1 cup parsley, chopped
2 lbs. raw ground turkey
1 1/2 cups bread crumbs
1 tsp. pepper
3 large egg whites, beaten lightly
Pinch of sage, thyme, and
   crushed red pepper

In saucepan, cook half of onion and all the garlic in oil until onion is softened. Add tomatoes, oregano, basil and wine. Simmer, stirring occasionally, for 15 minutes. In food processor, chop fine the remaining onion with bell pepper and zucchini. Combine all ingredients. Divide between 2 loaf pans and bake at 350° for 1 hour, 15 minutes. (A meat thermometer inserted in center of loaf should read 160 to 165°.) Let the baked meat loaf stand 5 to 10 minutes and it will be easier to slice. Yield: 8 to 10 servings.

▲ ▲ ▲

Turkey tetrazzini

Always popular after the holidays is turkey tetrazzini, which uses leftover turkey.
Of course, it can be made at any time with cooked turkey or chicken.

1 can cream of chicken or mushroom soup (undiluted)
2 cups cubed cooked turkey
1/2 cup grated Parmesan cheese
1 cup turkey or chicken stock or canned chicken broth
4 to 5 oz. spaghetti, cooked and drained
1 (10-oz.) pkg. frozen peas, thawed
1/2 tsp. Worcestershire sauce
1/2 tsp. salt
Dash pepper
1/4 cup toasted almonds (optional)
Paprika

Combine soup, turkey stock, cheese and cooked turkey in saucepan.
Mix well. Heat slowly, stirring until mixture comes to boil. Place half of
spaghetti, peas, Worcestershire sauce and seasonings (except paprika) in
shallow, 2-quart baking dish. Top with half of soup mixture. Repeat layers.
Sprinkle with almonds and paprika. Place under broiler, 4 inches from
heat, for 4 minutes, or until brown or bubbly, or heat 20 minutes at 350°,
until hot through. Sprinkle with additional Parmesan cheese and paprika.

▲ ▲ ▲

Peppy clam shells

A spicy clam mixture baked in individual seashells or dishes is a favorite of
Nancy Baker of Dandridge. She triples the recipe to serve six.

1/2 cup finely chopped onion	1/4 tsp. salt
1/2 cup finely chopped celery	Dash pepper
1/4 cup finely chopped green pepper	Dash Worcestershire sauce
4 Tbsp. melted butter	Lemon juice (2 tsp. to 1 Tbsp.)
2 Tbsp. flour	1/2 cup crushed Ritz crackers
2 Tbsp. freshly grated Parmesan	1 (7 1/2-oz.) can minced clams
Parmesan cheese (for topping)	1 Tbsp. melted butter

Cook onion, celery and green pepper in butter until tender, but not
brown. Stir in flour, cheese, seasonings and lemon juice. Add half of the
crackers and mix. Stir in undrained clams. Cook a few minutes, until
mixture thickens and bubbles. Divide evenly among 3 or 4 individual shell
baking dishes. Combine remaining cracker crumbs and butter and sprinkle
over top. Top with additional Parmesan cheese. Bake at 350° for 15
minutes. Don't overbake because clams will be tough. Yield: 2 servings.

▲ ▲ ▲
Seafood casserole

This is an easy casserole that can be put together after work if you have the seafood on hand.

1 (4.25-oz.) can baby shrimp
1 (6-oz.) can crabmeat
1 (6 1/2-oz.) can tuna
1 cup mayonnaise
1 egg
1 can cream of celery soup
2 1/2 cups cooked shell macaroni
1/2 medium onion, diced
1/2 medium green pepper, diced

Mix all ingredients and place in buttered 9-by-13-inch baking dish. Bake at 350° for 45 minutes.

If desired, top casserole with crushed croutons coated with melted butter or with buttered bread crumbs after casserole has baked for 30 minutes. Return to oven for final 15 minutes. Yield: 2 to 4 servings.

▲ ▲ ▲
Shrimp etouffee

Sarah Gose's Louisiana shrimp recipe came to her in Morristown via Mexico. She serves it over rice.

1 stick margarine
2 or 3 large onions, chopped
1 (8-oz.) can tomato sauce
10 drops Tabasco
Garlic salt, to taste
1 small bay leaf
1/2 cup beer
Pinch of tarragon
2 lbs. shelled and deveined shrimp or crayfish
Cooked rice

Stir fry onions in margarine until transparent. Add all other ingredients except shrimp and rice. Bring to a boil. Add shelled shrimp and simmer about 5 to 10 minutes to cook shrimp. Serve over cooked rice. Yield: 6 servings.

▲ ▲ ▲
Tuna and corn muffins

An easy supper dish is a cheesy-tuna mixture served over corn muffins.

1 (6 1/2 oz.) can tuna
2 garlic cloves, minced
1 medium onion, chopped
2 Tbsp. butter
2 Tbsp. flour
1/2 tsp. Worcestershire sauce
1 1/2 cups milk
2 cups shredded sharp cheddar cheese
2 Tbsp. mayonnaise
4 corn muffins, split
1/2 tsp. dill weed (optional)

Drain tuna. Stir fry garlic and onion in butter until onion is soft. Stir in flour and Worcestershire sauce until blended. Gradually stir in milk, whisking constantly while cooking until thickened. Remove from heat. Stir in cheese and mayonnaise. Add tuna.
To serve, spoon tuna mixture onto corn muffin halves. Garnish with dill, if desired. Yield: 2 servings.

▲ ▲ ▲
Tuna creole

Kenneth Badget of Knoxville prepared this special tuna dish when he was chef for the YWCA Values and Viewpoints lecture series.

1 (3 to 4-oz.) can mushrooms
1/4 cup chopped onion
1/4 cup chopped green pepper
2 Tbsp. butter or margarine
2 tsp. all-purpose flour
1/4 tsp. salt
Dash pepper
1/2 cup ketchup
1 (6 1/2 to 7 1/2-oz.) can tuna
3 cups hot cooked rice

Drain mushrooms and reserve liquid, adding enough water to make 1 cup. Set liquid aside. Saute mushrooms, onions and green pepper in butter until tender. Stir in flour, salt and pepper. Add mushroom liquid and ketchup. Heat slowly until mixture thickens. Add tuna and heat. Serve over hot rice. Yield: 4 servings.

▲ ▲ ▲

Cottage cheese croquettes

Marilyn Bowers, staff dietitian with the University of Tennessee Food Services Department, remembers making cottage cheese croquettes when she worked at Sophronia Strong cafeteria at UT. The croquettes were always popular and when a reader requested the recipe, Bowers worked it out for two servings.

3/4 cup cottage cheese
3/4 cup bread crumbs
3 Tbsp. chopped pecans
1/8 tsp. paprika
1 tsp. chopped onion
1 Tbsp. chopped green pepper
1/8 tsp. salt
Flour
1 egg, beaten
1/2 cup milk
Additional bread crumbs for coating
Sauce (recipe follows)

Combine cottage cheese, bread crumbs, chopped pecans, paprika, chopped onion, chopped green pepper and salt. Shape mixture into two cone-shaped croquettes. Roll croquettes in flour and then in beaten egg and milk, combined. Roll in additional bread crumbs until well coated.

Fry in deep fat fryer, 325°, until golden brown (2 to 3 minutes). Do not overcook.

Note: Croquettes are best when fried in deep fat fryer. Do not use shallow fat in skillet because croquettes will absorb too much fat. Though this is the traditional method of preparing croquettes, an alternative might be baking them at 350 to 400° until brown and warmed through.

Serve with sauce. Garnish with chopped parsley or cooked green peas. Yield: 2 servings.

Sauce:
1 Tbsp. all-purpose flour
1 Tbsp. margarine
3/4 cup milk
1/8 tsp. salt

Melt margarine. Add flour and cook and stir until well blended. Slowly stir in milk and salt. Cook until thickened.

▲ ▲ ▲

Fresh tomato sauce and pasta

News-Sentinel features editor Linda Felts Fields suggests serving this sauce over tri-colored fusili with a salad and French bread.

6 very ripe tomatoes
1 clove garlic, minced
1 Tbsp. olive oil
1/2 cup chopped onions
1/4 cup chopped green pepper
1/4 cup chopped parsley
1/2 cup sliced fresh mushrooms
6 leaves fresh basil, chopped, or 1/2 tsp. dried
Few sprigs fresh thyme or 1/4 tsp. dried
1/4 tsp. sugar (optional)
Salt and pepper to taste
Cooked pasta
Parmesan cheese

Peel and chop tomatoes. Mince garlic and saute in olive oil with green pepper and onion over medium heat. Lower heat and add chopped tomatoes, mushrooms, parsley and seasonings. Cover and simmer at least 15 minutes. Serve over pasta sprinkled generously with Parmesan cheese. Yield: 3 to 4 servings.

▲ ▲ ▲

Macaroni and cheese

Clara Mount of Knoxville sends a version of macaroni and cheese.

1/2 lb. macaroni
Salted water
1 cup cheese cubes
3 Tbsp. butter
1 tsp. salt

1/8 tsp. cayenne pepper
1/2 cup milk
1 egg
1/2 cup buttered bread crumbs

Boil macaroni in salted water until tender, about 20 minutes. Blanch in cold water to prevent macaroni from sticking together. Cover bottom of baking dish with layer of macaroni, a sprinkle of cheese cubes, bits of butter, salt and pepper. Continue until all is used, topping with cheese.

Mix milk and egg together. Pour over macaroni, cover top with bread crumbs. Bake in 350° oven until bubbly and top is brown.

▲ ▲ ▲

Spinach lasagna

This spinach lasagna is a favorite with our son, Chris Durman, who is a vegetarian. It is easy to fix and it freezes well. Our first sample of it came when News-Sentinel staff writer Sibyl Jefferson brought the dish to a gathering.

2 Tbsp. olive or salad oil

1 large onion, chopped

1 or 2 cloves garlic, minced

1 tsp. dried oregano

2 pkg. (10-oz. each) frozen chopped spinach, thawed and drained

1 can cream of celery soup

2 cups shredded sharp cheddar cheese

1 egg

1 (32-oz.) jar spaghetti sauce (or 4 cups homemade sauce)

1/2 cup dry red wine

9 lasagna noodles, cooked and drained

2 cups shredded mozzarella cheese

Cook onion and garlic in hot oil in large skillet until tender. (Do not let garlic brown.) Add oregano and stir. Add spinach and stir. Remove from heat and stir in soup, cheddar cheese and egg. Set aside.

In medium bowl, stir together spaghetti sauce and wine. Pour half the sauce mixture into 13-by-9-inch baking dish. Arrange 3 cooked lasagna noodles over sauce. Spread with half of the spinach filling. Sprinkle with a third of the mozzarella. Arrange 3 more noodles over cheese. Spread with remaining spinach mixture. Sprinkle with another third of the mozzarella. Top with remaining 3 noodles and remaining sauce.

Bake at 350° for 40 minutes or until hot and bubbly. Sprinkle with remaining mozzarella cheese. Bake 5 minutes more. Remove from oven and let stand 15 minutes before serving. Yield: 6 to 8 servings.

Desserts

▲ ▲ ▲
Desserts

▲ ▲ ▲
Apple cake

Bill Orr of Jefferson City prefers to use Granny Smith apples in this cake.

1 cup vegetable oil
2 cups sugar
3 eggs
3 cups chopped peeled apples
1 cup chopped pecans
2 1/2 cup all-purpose flour
1 tsp. salt
1 tsp. baking soda
2 tsp. baking powder

Topping:
1/2 cup margarine
1 cup brown sugar
1 can (about 1 cup) coconut
1/2 cup milk
1 tsp. vanilla

Combine shortening and sugar, blending well. Add eggs, apples and nuts. Sift together and add the dry ingredients. Batter will be stiff.

Pour batter into greased and floured tube or Bundt pan. Bake in preheated 350° oven 50 to 60 minutes. Remove from oven and cool 10 minutes before removing from pan by inverting it on a plate.

For topping: Blend first four ingredients in saucepan. Cook over low to medium heat. Remove from heat. Stir in vanilla. Apply topping while cake is hot. Let it soak in about 10 minutes, then spoon topping that runs onto plate back onto cake several times so topping will penetrate the cake.

▲ ▲ ▲
Banana split cake

Grady E. Griggs, Norris, sends a recipe for banana split cake.

3 cups graham cracker crumbs
1/4 cup butter, melted
1/4 cup sugar
2 cups confectioners' sugar
1/2 cup butter, softened
1 egg
1 tsp. vanilla

4 bananas
2 (10-oz.) pkg. frozen strawberries thawed and drained
1 (15-oz.) can crushed pineapple, drained
2 cups whipped cream
1 cup chopped nuts

Combine crumbs, melted butter and 1/4 cup sugar. Mix well and press into 14-by-9-by-2-inch baking dish. Cool for 1 hour or more. Beat together confectioners' sugar and butter. Add egg and vanilla and beat well. Spread evenly over crumb layer and chill for 1 hour. Slice bananas and place on egg layer. Drain strawberries and pineapple well and spread over bananas. Spread whipped cream on top and sprinkle with nuts. Chill until ready to serve. Yield: 12 servings.

▲ ▲ ▲

Better than sex cake

This cake has many variations — such as chocolate cake mix instead of yellow or a different flavor of pudding mix. Here's the recipe from Gladys Smith of Knoxville.

1 pkg. yellow butter cake mix
1 large (5-oz.) pkg. instant chocolate pudding mix
2/3 cup oil
2/3 cup sugar
1/3 cup water
4 eggs
1/2 pint sour cream
6 oz. chocolate morsels

Combine cake mix, pudding mix, oil, sugar and water. Add eggs, one at a time, using electric mixer. Stir in by hand the sour cream and chocolate morsels. Pour into well-greased Bundt or tube pan. Bake at 350° for 1 hour. Let cool before removing from pan. The cake is better made a day ahead.

▲ ▲ ▲

Pumpkin cheesecake

1 pkg. spice cake mix
1/2 cup butter or margarine, melted
3 (8-oz.) pkgs. cream cheese, softened
1 can sweetened condensed milk
1 (16-oz.) can pumpkin
4 eggs
1 Tbsp. pumpkin pie spice

Topping:
1 (2 1/2 oz.) pkg. sliced almonds
2 cups whipping cream, chilled
1/4 cup sugar

Preheat oven to 375°. Combine cake mix and melted butter in large bowl. Press into bottom of ungreased 10-inch springform pan.

For the filling, combine cream cheese and sweetened condensed milk in large bowl. Beat with electric mixer at high speed for 2 minutes. Add pumpkin, eggs and pumpkin pie spice. Beat at high speed 1 minute. Pour over prepared crust in pan. Bake for 65 to 70 minutes or until filling is set. Cool completely on a rack. Refrigerate 2 hours. Loosen cake from sides of pan. Remove sides of pan.

For the topping: Preheat oven to 300°. Toast almonds by spreading on baking sheet and baking for 4 to 5 minutes. Cool completely. Beat whipping cream in medium bowl until soft peaks form. Gradually add sugar, continuing to beat until stiff peaks form. Spread over top of chilled cake. Garnish with the toasted almonds. Refrigerate until ready to serve. Serves 8 to 12.

▲ ▲ ▲
Litton's cheesecake

Lynda Jones, who makes the desserts at Litton's Restaurant, Knoxville, shares a basic cheesecake recipe. It's one of the most popular desserts at Litton's.

3 (8-oz.) pkgs. cream cheese
1 to 1 1/4 cups granulated sugar
1 tsp. vanilla (or a liqueur, such as Grand Marnier or apricot brandy)
1/8 tsp. salt
3 extra large eggs
1 cup sour cream

Beat together with electric beater the cream cheese and sugar until the sugar is mixed through. Add vanilla and salt. Add eggs, one at a time, beating only until eggs are stirred in. Gently blend in sour cream.

Pour into cooled shortbread crust in 9-inch springform pan. Bake 1 hour to 1 hour and 15 minutes at 300°. Filling is done when it still jiggles a little in the center. If soupy in the center, continue baking or turn oven off and let cheesecake set about 15 minutes.

Shortbread crust:
1 stick butter
1/4 cup sugar
1 cup flour
1/2 to 1 tsp. flavoring (lemon rind or grated chocolate, chopped nuts or a liqueur)
1 egg yolk

Crumble butter and sugar together. Add flour, flavoring and egg yolk. Press into pan. Bake 10 minutes at 400°. Let cool before filling.

Apricot glaze:
1 cup apricot jam
1 Tbsp. apricot brandy

Combine in saucepan and heat gently. Spoon over cake just before serving or spoon over a slice of cake. Yield: 12 to 14 servings.

▲ ▲ ▲

Andes mint chocolate cake

Betsy Pickle of The News-Sentinel staff says this cake is great with Breyers mint chocolate chip ice cream.

1 sour cream chocolate or devil's food cake mix
20 to 30 Andes Creme de Menthe candies

Prepare cake mix according to package directions and pour into two layer baking pans.

Chop mints into crumb-sized pieces. Sprinkle half across surface of each pan, avoiding the sides of the pans. Push crumbs into batter with knife or spatula. Bake, then cool 10 minutes in pan. Apply frosting while cake is still warm.

Frosting:
15 to 20 Andes Creme de Menthe candies
1 can chocolate frosting (any kind except milk chocolate)

Line bottom and sides of microwaveable bowl with single layer of mints. Heat in microwave until thoroughly melted; stir to mix mint with chocolate. Spread melted candy over top and sides of each cake layer. Cool until hardened. When coating is hard, apply frosting to bottom layer. Add second layer, frost top and sides of cake. Serve at room temperature or chilled.

▲ ▲ ▲

Chocolate bar cake

The chocolate bar cake at Grady's Goodtimes, Knoxville, is often requested. At the restaurant, the cake is served with vanilla ice cream and a rich fudge sauce. Darlene Kerley of Knoxville says she makes this version that is like Grady's.

1 cup butter	**1 cup buttermilk**
2 cups sugar	**1/2 tsp. baking soda**
4 eggs	**8 (1.65-oz.) milk chocolate candy bars**
2 1/2 cups all-purpose	**1 (8-oz.) can chocolate syrup**
flour, sifted	**2 tsp. vanilla**

Cream together the butter and sugar. Add eggs, 1 at a time. Dissolve soda in buttermilk and add to sugar mixture alternately with flour. Melt candy bars in chocolate syrup in saucepan and add to sugar mixture. Stir in vanilla. Pour into greased and floured Bundt pan. Bake at 300° for 2 hours to 2 hours, 20 minutes, until cake tests done. Cool on wire rack about 15 minutes. Remove from pan.

Note: Kerley says the secret is the long baking time. She uses 1 1/2 sticks butter and 1/2 stick margarine to make the 1 cup shortening and she uses White Lily all-purpose flour.

▲ ▲ ▲

Chocolate covered cherry cake

Mrs. Robert B. Winsbro, Kingston, sends a recipe for chocolate covered cherry cake in answer to a request. She says the cake needs to be made with a regular cake mix, not one containing pudding nor one that requires butter to be added.

1 tsp. almond flavoring
1 can cherry pie filling
2 eggs
1 (2-layer size) pkg. devil's food
  cake mix

Frosting:
1 cup granulated sugar
5 Tbsp. butter or margarine
1/3 cup undiluted evaporated milk
1 (6-oz.) pkg. semisweet
  chocolate morsels
1 tsp. vanilla (optional)

Mix almond flavoring into cherry pie filling. Beat eggs in large bowl. Add cherry pie filling. Add cake mix and stir well with a spoon (a mixer tends to chop up the cherries) until evenly moist. Do not add the water called for on package of cake mix.

Pour into greased and floured 9-by-13-inch pan (or jelly roll pan if you want brownie thickness). Bake at 350° for 25 to 30 minutes (or 20 to 30 minutes in jelly roll pan).

For frosting: Bring sugar, butter and milk to a boil and boil for 1 minute, stirring occasionally. Remove from heat and stir in chocolate morsels until melted. Add vanilla. Pour over cake while still in pan. Let stand until cool.

▲ ▲ ▲

Chocolate eclair cake

Chocolate eclair cake is a popular dessert and many readers contribute the recipe when someone requests it. This one's from Faye Seal, Maynardville.

1 box graham crackers
2 small or 1 large pkg. vanilla or french vanilla instant pudding mix
3 cups milk
8-oz. carton whipped topping
1 can milk chocolate frosting or 1 jar chocolate ice cream topping

Line bottom of 9-by-13-inch pan with whole graham crackers. Mix pudding and milk on low speed of electric mixer. By hand, fold in whipped topping. Spoon half of pudding mixture over graham crackers. Repeat layer of graham crackers and remaining pudding mixture. Top pudding with third layer of whole graham crackers. Spread frosting over top. Refrigerate 3 to 4 hours or overnight.

Note: Chocolate frosting will spread easier if can is set in hot water for a few minutes, then stirred.

▲ ▲ ▲

Chocolate mound cake

Sharon Price, Kingston, says this is her husband's favorite birthday cake. She recommends following it in the steps given.

For frosting:
1/2 cup cocoa
1/2 cup milk
2 cups sugar
1/4 cup light corn syrup
1 stick margarine
1 tsp. vanilla

For filling:
1 cup sugar
1 cup milk
30 large marshmallows
1 (14-oz.) pkg. coconut
1 tsp. vanilla
1 pkg. devil's food cake mix

To make frosting: Bring to a boil the cocoa, 1/2 cup milk, 2 cups sugar and corn syrup. Remove from heat and add margarine and 1 teaspoon vanilla. Blend together well. Put in refrigerator until very cold.

To make filling: Heat 1 cup sugar and 1 cup milk until hot and sugar is melted. Add marshmallows and stir until all are melted. Bring to a boil and add coconut and 1 teaspoon vanilla. Stir together well and set aside.

Prepare cake mix according to package directions to make 2 layers and cool. Slice each layer in half lengthwise to make 4 layers. Arrange cake as follows: Place 1 layer of cake on plate. Top with coconut filling. Top with next layer of cake and coconut filling. Top with third layer of cake and coconut filling. Place last layer on top of all.

Remove frosting from refrigerator. Put some onto the middle of the cake. Frosting softens fast and will run down the sides. Continue doing this until all frosting is used and the cake is covered. You may need to put the cake on a platter that has a fluted edge so the frosting does not run off.

The cake must be kept in the refrigerator and freezes well, too. It is best to make the cake the day before and let it set overnight.

▲ ▲ ▲
Dirt cake

*Frances Fernandez of Detroit sends a recipe for dirt cake, a cross between
pudding and cheesecake. It is made in flower pots or plastic sand buckets, which
also can be used to decorate the table. The cake can be decorated with flowers
and gummy worms. A plastic garden trowel can be used for serving.*

1/2 cup butter, softened
1 (8-oz.) pkg. cream cheese, softened
1/2 to 1 cup confectioners' sugar, sifted
3 1/2 cups milk
2 (3 1/2-oz.) pkgs. instant vanilla or chocolate pudding
12 oz. frozen whipped topping, partially thawed
1 (7-inch) flower pot or 10 small flower pots
1 (20-oz.) pkg. chocolate sandwich cookies, crushed

Wash plastic pots with soapy water. If clay pot is used, rinse with clear
water and wipe dry. (Soap will absorb into the clay.) To sterilize a clay pot,
set it on a cookie sheet and place it in 350° oven for 20 minutes.
In medium size bowl, mix butter, cream cheese and sugar with a mixer.
In a second medium bowl, mix the milk and pudding. Add the whipped
topping to the pudding mixture. Combine the two mixtures.
Cover the bottom of each flower pot with a plastic lid, foil or plastic
wrap. Layer cookie crumbs and creamy mixture, making several layers of
each and ending with cookies on top. Cover and refrigerate several hours.
Serves 8 to 10.

▲ ▲ ▲
Fatman cake

2 cups self-rising flour
1 (1-lb.) pkg. brown sugar
1/2 cup granulated sugar
4 eggs
2 sticks margarine, melted
1 tsp. vanilla

Combine the cooled melted margarine with the eggs and sugar. Blend
in the remaining ingredients and pour into a well-greased 9-by-13-by-2-
inch pan. Bake for 10 minutes at 350° and then open the oven door and
shake the pan several times. Continue baking for 20 more minutes at
350°. Serve warm. Yield: 10 to 12 servings.
The cake has a brownie-like texture and requires no icing or glaze.

▲ ▲ ▲

Applesauce fruitcake

Jimmie Sue Campbell, Lenoir City, makes this fruitcake using canned applesauce. The recipe came from her mother, Eulah Mae Fine, who always made her own applesauce for the cake.

4 cups applesauce
2 heaping tsp. baking soda
2 cups sugar
1 cup solid shortening
4 cups all-purpose flour
1 tsp. nutmeg
1 tsp. cinnamon

1 tsp. allspice
1 box seedless raisins
1 pkg. figs, cut up
1 pkg. chopped sugared dates
1 large pkg. mixed candied fruit
1 cup chopped pecans

Heat applesauce until it is steaming hot. Add soda. When well dissolved, stir in sugar and shortening. Put 1/4 cup of the flour in a separate container and add fruit and nuts, coating fruits well with flour. Sift remaining flour with spices and stir into sugar mixture. Stir in fruit. Spoon into greased and floured tube pan and bake approximately 2 to 2 1/2 hours at 275°. If cake starts to brown, cover it with foil and finish baking.

Remove from oven. Let set 10 to 15 minutes and remove from pan. Wrap cake tightly in foil to store.

Cake freezes well.

▲ ▲ ▲

Mystery fruitcake

Lynda Presley, Sweetwater, says this fruitcake is one of the best —and easiest!

1 pkg. yellow cake mix
4 cups mixed candied fruit
1 (8-oz.) pkg. red candied cherries
1 (8-oz.) pkg. green candied cherries
1 1/2 cups raisins
2 cups chopped pecans
1 (8-oz.) pkg. chopped dates
1 (7.5-oz.) pkg. fluffy white frosting mix

Prepare cake mix as directed on package. Let cool. Break in small pieces. Place in large bowl or pan. Add all fruits, nuts, raisins and dates. Prepare frosting mix as directed on package. Pour over other ingredients and mix, using your hands. Line tube pan with aluminum foil. Pack cake in pan, cover with foil and refrigerate 24 hours before unmolding to serve.

▲ ▲ ▲

Unbaked fruitcake

From the University of Tennessee Agriculture Extension Service comes an oft-requested recipe for a no-bake fruitcake.

2 cups pecans, chopped
1 lb. vanilla wafers, finely crushed
1/4 lb. candied cherries, chopped
1/4 lb. dates, chopped
1/4 lb. candied pineapple, chopped
1 can sweetened condensed milk

Combine all ingredients. Mix by hand. Press into wax paper-lined loaf pan. Decorate as desired. Refrigerate until firm.

▲ ▲ ▲

Graham cracker crumb cake

Janice Moody, Kingston, sends a recipe for graham cracker cake.

2 cups sugar
2 sticks margarine, softened
4 eggs, room temperature
1 pkg. (4 cup) graham cracker crumbs
1 tsp. baking powder
1 cup milk, room temperature
1 cup coconut
1 cup chopped pecans or black walnuts
1 tsp. vanilla

Frosting:
1 cup sugar
4 tsp. all-purpose flour
2 1/2 cups drained crushed pineapple

Beat together sugar and margarine. Add eggs and remaining ingredients. Pour into 3 greased layer cake pans. Bake at 300° for 40 minutes or until firm and cake tests done. Cool and remove from pans. Fill and frost.
To make frosting: Combine ingredients and cook until thick. If mixture doesn't get thick, add a little more flour, beating well. Cool about 10 minutes before spreading between cake layers and on top. Let cake age 3 to 5 days. Store in cool place, but do not refrigerate.

▲▲▲

Hawaiian cake

On a flight home from Hawaii, Gladys Smith of Knoxville chatted about recipes with her seatmate. The woman gave her a good cake recipe, easy to make, and in memory of the trip, Smith named it Hawaiian cake.

1 pkg. Duncan Hines butter cake mix
3 eggs
1/3 cup oil
1 small can mandarin oranges
  with juice

Pineapple frosting:
1 (3-oz.) pkg. vanilla pudding mix
1 (15-oz.) can crushed pineapple
  with juice
9 oz. whipped topping

Combine cake mix, eggs, oil and oranges with juice. Beat with electric mixer until well blended, approximately 2 minutes. Pour into well-greased and floured 9-by-13-inch pan (or two 9-inch or three 8-inch pans). Bake at 350° for 35 to 40 minutes for sheet cake or 25 to 30 minutes for layers. Cool and frost.

To make frosting: Mix instant pudding mix with pineapple until well blended. Fold in whipped topping. Frost cake.

▲▲▲

Hot milk cake

This old-fashioned cake is from Grace Zachary.

2 eggs
1 cup sugar
1 cup all-purpose flour
1 rounded tsp. baking powder
Dash salt
1 tsp. vanilla
1 Tbsp. butter
1/2 cup milk

Frosting:
3 Tbsp. butter
2 Tbsp. cream
5 Tbsp. brown sugar
1/2 cup chopped nuts

Beat eggs. Add sugar gradually and beat for 5 minutes. Add flour mixed with baking powder and salt. Add vanilla. Melt butter; add milk to butter and let it get warm. Add to first mixture. Pour into greased 9-inch square pan and bake at 375° for 30 minutes. (Double ingredients and add 15 minutes to baking time for a 9-by-13-inch pan.

To prepare frosting: Melt butter. Add cream, brown sugar and chopped nuts. Mix well and bring to boil. Spread on cake. If desired, place under broiler to brown lightly. You can add about 1/2 cup coconut.

▲ ▲ ▲
Hurricane cake

Duff's Restaurant serves hurricane cake and the recipe is often requested. The restaurant doesn't give out the recipe, but readers have sent copy-cat versions.

1 1/2 cups sugar
2 cups all-purpose flour
2 tsp. baking soda
2 eggs
1/4 cup Coffee-mate
1/4 cup water
1 (16-oz.) can chopped peaches
Juice from 16-oz. can peaches

Topping:
1 1/2 cups milk
1 cup sugar
Pinch salt
2 sticks margarine
3 Tbsp. cornstarch

Combine cake ingredients in mixing bowl and blend. Mixture will be lumpy. Pour into lightly greased and floured 9-by-13-by-2-inch pan and bake at 325° for 35 minutes or until cake tests done.

To make topping: Combine milk, sugar, salt and margarine in saucepan and bring to a boil. Boil until slightly thick. Mix a little of the topping with the cornstarch, stirring to blend well. Return cornstarch mixture to saucepan and cook until mixture thickens, stirring constantly. Cut cake in squares and pour topping over the cake.

▲ ▲ ▲
Jam cake

Gladys Smith shares a recipe for old-fashioned jam cake and caramel frosting.

1/2 cup shortening
1 cup sugar
4 eggs, well beaten
1 1/2 cups thick jam, jelly or preserves (blackberry, strawberry)
2 1/2 cups all-purpose flour
1 tsp. soda
3/4 tsp. salt
1 tsp. cinnamon
1/2 tsp. allspice
1 tsp. nutmeg
1/4 cup buttermilk

Cream together shortening and sugar. Add eggs and jam. Beat thoroughly. Add flour, soda, salt and spices alternately with buttermilk to first mixture. Beat thoroughly. Pour into greased Bundt or tube pan. Bake 45 minutes at 375°. Cool; remove from pan and frost.

(Please see following page for caramel frosting recipe.)

Caramel frosting for jam cake (see previous page):
1 cup granulated sugar
1/2 tsp. soda
1/2 stick margarine
1/2 tsp. vanilla
1/2 cup brown sugar
Pinch salt
1/2 cup buttermilk

Mix all ingredients in large saucepan. Bring to boil, then cook slowly to soft ball stage (236° on candy thermometer). Cool and beat until creamy. Spread on cake.

▲ ▲ ▲

Ooey-gooey

"Ooey-gooey" and "fatman cake" (page 129) are simple, but "simply delicious," says Rose Armbrister of Knoxville.

1 pkg. yellow cake mix
1 stick margarine, melted
3 eggs
1 (12-oz.) pkg. semisweet chocolate morsels
1 (8-oz.) pkg. cream cheese
1 (1-lb.) pkg. confectioners' sugar

Combine cake mix, melted margarine and 1 egg. Press into 9-by-13-by-2-inch greased pan. Pour chocolate chips over the mixture. Blend the remaining eggs, confectioners' sugar and cream cheese on medium speed until well blended. Pour over chips. Bake for 40 minutes at 350°. Chill.

▲ ▲ ▲

Orange or lemon crumb cake

Jane Hallen of Jefferson City serves an orange crumb cake from a recipe that came from Lucille Tinsley, also of Jefferson City. It needs to be made ahead and refrigerated 24 hours. The cake also can be made into a lemon version.

1 pkg. orange (or lemon) cake mix
1 (8-oz.) container whipped topping
1 (6-oz.) can frozen orange juice or lemonade, undiluted
1 can sweetened condensed milk
1 small can coconut, or as much as desired

Prepare cake mix according to package directions, baking it in a 9-by-13-inch greased pan. Let cake cool, then cut it in half.

Mix together whipped topping, orange juice and sweetened condensed milk. Divide mixture into two parts.

Crumble half of cake in bottom of 9-by-13-inch pan. Press crumbs down with a fork. Spread half of topping on the cake. Repeat with other half of cake, again pressing the crumbs down with a fork. Spread remaining topping over crumbs. Sprinkle with coconut. Refrigerate 24 hours.

▲ ▲ ▲

Orange slice cake

From Johnnie Rodgers, New Market, comes this cake.

2 sticks butter or margarine
2 cups sugar
4 eggs
3 1/2 cups all-purpose flour
1 cup chopped pecans
1/2 bag orange slices candy, cut in small pieces
1 pkg. dates, cut in pieces
1 tsp. soda
1/2 cup buttermilk
1 cup coconut

Orange slice topping:
2/3 cup orange juice
2 cups confectioners' sugar

Beat together butter and sugar; add eggs, one at a time. Roll pecans, candy and dates in 1/2 cup of the flour. Add rest of flour and soda to butter-sugar mixture alternately with buttermilk, coconut and candy mixture. Pour into greased loaf pan and bake at 250° for 2 hours. Mix topping ingredients and pour over cake while hot. Let cake set in pan overnight.

▲ ▲ ▲

Baptist pound cake

Another favorite is Baptist pound cake from Mildred Tate of Knoxville. It starts in a cold oven. The vanilla-butter-nut flavoring is a combination available in grocery stores.

3 cups sugar
1 stick butter or margarine
1/2 cup solid shortening
5 eggs
3 cups all-purpose flour

1/2 tsp. baking powder
Pinch of salt
1 cup sweet milk
1 tsp. vanilla
1 Tbsp vanilla-butter-nut flavoring

Beat together sugar, butter and shortening. Add eggs, one at a time and beat well after each. Sift flour, baking powder and salt together and add alternately with milk to first mixture. Add flavorings.

Grease and flour Bundt pan (or 10-inch tube pan or large loaf pan). Pour mixture into pan. Place in cold oven, turn heat to 350° and bake for 1 hour and 15 minutes, or until cake tests done. Let stand for 3 to 5 minutes before removing from pan.

▲ ▲ ▲

Four-flavor pound cake

Brona Maddox, Jefferson City, makes a four-flavoring pound cake.

2 sticks margarine, softened
1/2 cup solid shortening
2 3/4 cups sugar
5 eggs
3 1/2 cups all-purpose flour
1/2 tsp. salt
3/4 tsp. baking powder
1 cup milk
1/2 tsp. almond flavoring
1 tsp. orange flavoring
1/2 tsp. lemon flavoring
2 tsp. vanilla

Lemon glaze:
1 1/2 cups confectioners' sugar
2 or 3 Tbsp. skim milk
3/4 tsp. vanilla
1 Tbsp. lemon juice

Combine margarine and shortening with sugar, beating well. Add eggs, one at a time. Sift together dry ingredients and add alternately with milk and flavorings to sugar mixture. Pour into well-greased tube pan and bake in preheated 350° oven for 60 to 75 minutes or until cake tests done.

Cool cake in pan on rack 10 to 15 minutes; remove from pan. While cake is warm, pour glaze over cake. Wrap tightly in foil or plastic wrap.

To make glaze: Combine ingredients. Drizzle over top of warm cake.

▲ ▲ ▲
Lemon pound cake

Lemon pound cake is sold at Ham 'N' Goodies in Knoxville and is a favorite. Edna Hiers, Powell, contributes a recipe that came from Jewell Langley of Powell.

1 lb. butter or margarine, softened
2 cups sugar
6 eggs, at room temperature
1 can sweetened condensed milk
2 Tbsp. fresh lemon juice
2 Tbsp. vanilla-butter-nut flavoring
1/4 tsp. salt
3 cups all-purpose flour

Lemon glaze:
3/4 stick unsalted butter, melted
1 cup confectioners' sugar
2 Tbsp. fresh lemon juice

Beat together margarine and sugar. Add eggs, one at a time. Beat well after each addition. Add sweetened condensed milk, lemon juice, flavoring and salt. Add flour, 1 cup at a time, mixing well after each addition. Pour into greased and floured tube pan and bake in preheated 325° oven 1 hour and 45 minutes. Remove from oven and let cake set about 5 minutes. Remove from pan.

Prepare glaze by melting butter over low heat. Stir in sugar and lemon juice. Pour over cake while cake is hot. If desired, wrap cake in plastic wrap. It will stay fresh for days.

▲ ▲ ▲
Sour cream pound cake

From Rikki Traylor of Knoxville comes this sour cream pound cake. Try it with fresh strawberries. Slice the cake, top with a layer of sliced and sweetened strawberries, then with whipped cream. Repeat layers.

1/2 lb. butter (no substitute)
2 1/2 cups granulated sugar
6 whole eggs
3 cups all-purpose flour

1/4 tsp. soda
1 cup sour cream
1 tsp. vanilla

Beat together butter and sugar with electric mixer. Add eggs, one at a time. Sift flour and soda and add to butter mixture alternately with sour cream and vanilla. Pour into greased and floured tube or 10-inch Bundt pan and bake 1 hour and 15 minutes in preheated 325° oven (or until cake tests done). Cool 15 minutes, then remove from pan.

Note: Traylor uses White Lily all-purpose flour to make the cake.

▲ ▲ ▲

Strawberry pound cake

Pink and pretty is the strawberry pound cake from Janice Oster of Knoxville. There are not fresh berries in the cake, but fresh strawberries may be used to garnish the cake.

1 pkg. strawberry cake mix
1 pkg. (3-oz.) instant vanilla pudding
1/3 cup vegetable oil
1 cup water
4 eggs

Preheat oven to 350°. Generously grease and flour tube pan. Blend all ingredients in large bowl; beat at medium speed for 2 minutes. Pour into pan and bake for 50 to 60 minutes. Cool cake in pan 25 minutes, then invert onto serving plate.

▲ ▲ ▲

White chocolate pound cake

Gertie Porter of Knoxville serves this cake with fresh strawberries.

1 cup shortening
2 1/2 cups sugar
6 eggs
1/4 lb. white chocolate
1/4 cup hot water
3 cups sifted all-purpose flour
1 1/2 tsp. baking powder
1/2 tsp. salt
3/4 cup milk
1 tsp. vanilla

White chocolate glaze:
1/4 cup margarine
1/2 cup evaporated milk
2 cups sugar
1/4 lb. white chocolate
1 tsp. vanilla

Combine shortening and sugar with electric mixer, beating until light and fluffy. Add eggs, one at a time, beating well after each addition. Melt white chocolate in hot water in top of double boiler set over hot water. Cool and add to sugar mixture. Combine flour, baking powder and salt. Add to creamed mixture alternately with milk. Mix well after each addition. Stir in vanilla.

Pour batter into greased and floured tube pan. Bake at 325° for 1 hour and 15 minutes or until cake tests done. Cool 10 minutes, remove from pan. Spoon white chocolate glaze over top.

To prepare glaze: Mix margarine, milk, sugar and white chocolate in heavy saucepan over low heat. Stir constantly. Boil 1 minute. Remove from heat. Add vanilla and beat until thick. Pour over cool cake.

▲ ▲ ▲

* White and light pound cake

Joan Cohn of Knoxville decided to turn a pound cake into a low cholesterol dessert. She uses egg whites and not the yolks. She also uses unsalted margarine, not butter. She varies the cake with cocoa and dark brown sugar in a second version below.

3 3/4 cups sifted all-purpose flour	2 cups plus 2 Tbsp. sugar
1 tsp. salt	1 1/4 cups egg whites
1 1/2 tsp. baking powder	1 tsp. vanilla
4 Tbsp. confectioners' sugar	1 tsp. lemon flavoring
2 sticks plus 6 Tbsp. unsalted	1/4 tsp. almond flavoring
margarine	

Sift flour once. Measure and add baking powder and salt. Sift three times. Stir in confectioners' sugar. Beat margarine until creamy. Add sugar gradually and beat until light and fluffy. Add dry ingredients gradually. Add unbeaten egg whites, 1/4 cup at a time, beating well after each addition. Add vanilla, lemon and almond flavoring and beat vigorously.

Line the bottom of 10-inch tube pan with two thicknesses of waxed paper. Grease with oil. Pour in batter and bake at 300° for 30 minutes; turn oven to 350° and continue baking for 30 minutes. You may need to add an extra 15 minutes before cake tests done.

Let cake cool completely in pan. Run a knife around the cake where it touches the tube. Turn out of pan and immediately flip back over so top will be back on top, not upside down.

▲ ▲ ▲

Cocoa streusel pound cake

6 Tbsp. sugar
3 Tbsp. cocoa
2 Tbsp. dark brown sugar
Chopped nuts

Combine ingredients.

Pour 1/3 of batter from white pound cake into pan. Cover with half of streusel mix, 1/3 more batter, remainder of streusel, rest of batter. Bake as directed for white pound cake.

▲ ▲ ▲

Punch bowl cake

Betty Hancock's punch bowl cake is best if made a day ahead and chilled overnight. Cover tightly with transparent wrap and foil. Store in refrigerator.

1 pkg. yellow (or white) cake mix
1 large pkg. instant vanilla pudding mix
1 or 2 (16-oz.) cans crushed pineapple
1 or 2 cans cherry pie filing
1 (8-oz.) carton whipped topping
3/4 cup coconut
1 cup chopped pecans

Prepare cake as directed on package. Bake in 9-by-13-inch pan. Cool and break into small pieces. Prepare instant pudding as directed and chill.

Layer, half at a time, in punch bowl: cake pieces, crushed pineapple and juice, cherry pie filling, prepared instant pudding, whipped topping, coconut and pecans. Chill.

▲ ▲ ▲

Punch bowl cake II

Nancy Ridings' version of punch bowl cake is made with angel food cake and a variety of fruits.

1 large angel food cake
1 (16-oz.) carton whipped topping, thawed
1 (3-oz.) pkg. vanilla instant pudding mix
1 (3-oz.) pkg. strawberry instant pudding mix
1 (16-oz.) can sliced peaches, drained
1 (16-oz.) can pineapple chunks, drained
1 (16-oz.) can fruit cocktail, drained
1 1/2 cups strawberries (drained, if frozen)
1 can coconut
1 cup nuts
1 large jar maraschino cherries, drained

Crumble half of cake in punch bowl. Prepare vanilla and strawberry puddings according to package directions. Add vanilla pudding over cake layer. Layer all the peaches on top of pudding, then all the pineapple. Add half the whipped topping, half the coconut, half the nuts and half the drained maraschino cherries. Add remainder of cake, strawberry pudding, fruit cocktail and strawberries. Spread remainder of whipped topping over all. Add remaining coconut, nuts and cherries. Chill until ready to serve.

▲ ▲ ▲

Rum cake

Ada Clonts, Knoxville, has been making a rum cake for the holiday season for 30 years. The recipe came from her mother, Maude Bowers.

1 pkg. yellow cake mix with pudding
4 eggs
1/2 cup evaporated milk
1/2 cup vegetable oil
1/2 cup dark rum
Maraschino or candied cherries (for garnish)
Nuts (for garnish)
Whipped topping (for garnish)

Glaze:
1 stick butter
1/4 cup cold water
1 cup granulated sugar
1/2 cup dark rum

Combine cake mix, eggs, milk, oil and rum. Pour into greased and lightly floured Bundt cake pan. Bake in 325° oven for 55 minutes to 1 hour. Let cake set 10 minutes and remove from pan. While cake is still warm, punch holes in two circles around center, about 1 inch apart.

To make glaze: Bring butter, water and sugar to a boil Simmer 5 to 7 minutes. Cool while cake bakes. When cool, add rum. Drizzle glaze over top of cake, saving 1/4 cup. Tilt cake slightly and pour glaze onto sides of cake and down the top again.

Decorate with cherries and nuts. Drizzle with remaining glaze. Make two circles on cake with whipped topping, one around the holes and one at outside.

▲ ▲ ▲

Easy stack cake

JoAn Burnette of Knoxville gets rave reviews over her easily assembled apple stack cake. She buys the cake layers at Fountain City Bakery. They are sold in sets of six, but she uses nine layers so she buys two sets and freezes the other three layers to combine next time with a set of six. To make it even easier she purchases apple butter and chunky applesauce to combine for the filling.

6 to 9 stack cake layers
1 (29-oz.) jar apple butter
1/2 of a 25-oz. jar chunky applesauce
Allspice to taste, if desired

Combine apple butter with applesauce. Warm slightly in microwave or in saucepan. Add extra allspice, if desired. Spread between cake layers. Let cake stand a day before cutting it.

This is enough for 6 to 9 layers; double the filling for a larger cake.

▲ ▲ ▲

Stack cake

Margaret Hatmaker of LaFollette wins awards with this "from scratch" version.

2 cups sugar	Apple filling:
1 cup butter	1 lb. dried apples
2 eggs	1 cup brown sugar
1 tsp. vanilla	1/2 cup granulated sugar
1/2 cup buttermilk	2 tsp. cinnamon
6 cups all-purpose flour	1/2 tsp. cloves
1 tsp. salt	1/2 tsp. allspice
1 tsp. soda	
3 tsp. baking powder	

Combine sugar, butter, eggs and vanilla. Add buttermilk. Add flour, salt, soda and baking powder. Mix all together, kneading to form soft biscuit dough. Divide into 7 parts for 7 layers. Line round layer cake pans with wax paper. Pat dough in pans, very thin. Bake 6 to 7 minutes at 450°. Remove from pan and cool. Stack layers with filling. Let cake stand one day before cutting.

To make filling: Let apples set overnight or all day in warm water. Then rinse well. Place in saucepan and add no more water. Cover and let steam, stirring every 5 or 10 minutes, until tender. Add sugars and spices and cook 30 to 45 minutes more. Cool before putting between cake layers.

▲ ▲ ▲

Texas tornado cake

Another version of hurricane cake (recipe, page 133) is Texas tornado cake.

1 1/2 cups granulated sugar	Icing:
2 eggs	8 Tbsp. butter
2 cups canned fruit cocktail	3/4 cup sugar
2 tsp. baking soda	1/2 cup evaporated milk
2 cups all-purpose flour	1 cup flaked coconut
1/4 cup brown sugar	
1 cup chopped nuts	

In large bowl, combine sugar, eggs, fruit cocktail (including juice), baking soda and flour. Mix on low speed of electric mixer until well blended. Pour into lightly greased and floured 9-by-13-by-2-inch pan. Combine brown sugar and nuts and sprinkle evenly over batter. Bake at 325° for 40 minutes, until cake puffs up and tests done.

To make icing: In small pan, combine butter, sugar and milk. Boil 2 minutes. Remove from heat. Stir in coconut. Spoon over hot cake as soon as cake is removed from oven. Cut cake in squares when cool.

▲ ▲ ▲

Vanilla wafer cake

A request for vanilla wafer cake brought recipes from all over the area.

1 cup butter or margarine
2 cups granulated sugar
6 eggs
1 (12-oz.) pkg. vanilla wafers, crushed
1/2 cup milk
1 (7-oz.) pkg. or can flaked coconut
1 cup chopped pecans

Preheat oven to 300°. Beat butter and sugar until light and fluffy. Add eggs one at a time. Beat well after each addition. Add wafer crumbs alternately with milk, beginning and ending with crumbs. Fold in coconut and pecans. Pour into greased 10-inch tube pan or Bundt pan. Bake at 300° for 1 hour and 30 minutes or at 275° for 2 hours, until cake tests done.
If desired, add 1 teaspoon vanilla or 1/4 teaspoon almond flavoring. Frost vanilla wafer cake with cream cheese icing or caramel frosting:

Cream cheese icing:
1 (8-oz.) pkg. cream cheese
1 stick butter or margarine
1 pkg. confectioners' sugar
1 tsp. vanilla
1/2 cup chopped pecans

Melt margarine. Beat in softened cream cheese. Add confectioners' sugar, vanilla and pecans.

Caramel frosting:
1/2 cup butter
1 cup brown sugar
1/4 cup cream
1/2 cup sifted confectioners' sugar

Melt butter in heavy skillet on low heat. Blend in brown sugar and cream, stirring constantly. Bring to boil and cook until sugar is completely dissolved, about 1 minute. Remove from heat. Transfer to a bowl and cool to lukewarm, 110 degrees. Gradually add confectioners' sugar, beating until blended after each addition. Continue to beat until thick enough to spread.

▲ ▲ ▲

Watergate cake

Kay Zinn sends a recipe for Watergate cake.

1 pkg. white cake mix
1 (3-oz.) pkg. instant pistachio pudding
1 cup oil
1 cup 7-Up
3 eggs

Frosting:
1 (3-oz.) pkg. instant pistachio pudding
1 pkg. Dream Whip (2 envelopes)
1 1/2 cups milk
Coconut (optional)

Combine cake mix, pudding, oil, 7-Up and eggs. Pour into 9-by-13-inch greased and floured pan. Bake at 350° for 40 minutes or until cake tests done.

To make frosting: Combine pudding, dry whipped topping and milk. Beat until stiff enough to spread. Spread on cake. Sprinkle lightly with coconut, if desired.

Keep cake refrigerated.

▲ ▲ ▲

Apples and cheese

News-Sentinel editorial assistant Donna Colburn makes a delicious apple recipe that she often takes to parties. It's easy to prepare.

2 sticks margarine or butter
1 lb. Velveeta cheese
2 1/2 cups self-rising flour
2 cups sugar
2 (20-oz.) cans sliced apples with juice
Cinnamon, to taste

Combine butter, cheese, flour and sugar in saucepan and cook until butter is melted. Mix will be thick and lumpy. Put apples in bottom of 9-by-13-inch dish; sprinkle with cinnamon and cover with cheese mixture.

Bake at 350° for 30 minutes. Yield: 10 to 12 servings.

▲ ▲ ▲

Old-fashioned apple pie

Lon Sutton of Sevierville, winner of the sixth annual Tennessee Apple Festival apple pie contest at Sevierville, says his recipe is traditional. Try making it with a couple of different types of apples for an interesting taste.

6 to 8 apples	**Pie pastry:**
1 cup granulated sugar	2 cups all-purpose flour
2 Tbsp. all-purpose flour	1 tsp. salt
2 tsp. apple pie spice	1/2 cup solid shortening
1 stick margarine	7 Tbsp. cold water
Pastry for 2-crust pie	

To make pie pastry: In mixing bowl combine flour and salt. With pastry blender or two knives, cut in shortening until mixture resembles coarse meal. Sprinkle water over mixture, a tablespoon at a time. Mix lightly with fork until all flour is moistened. With hands, gather dough into a ball. Divide in half for top and bottom pastry.

Line pie plate with half the pastry. Mix apples, sugar, flour and spice in large bowl. Pour apples over pastry in pie plate. Rinse mixing bowl with about 2/3 cup cold water and pour over apples. Slice part of margarine on top of apples.

Roll out remaining pastry and place on apples. Make 3 slashes in crust. Dot pastry with margarine and sprinkle with sugar. Bake at 400° for 45 minutes to 1 hour.

▲ ▲ ▲

* Sugar-free apple pie

Mary Lee Roseberry of Athens won second place in one of the Tennessee Apple Festival pie contests with this sugar free pie.

1 (12-oz.) can frozen apple juice (no sugar added)	1/2 tsp. nutmeg
	7 cups sliced, peeled apples
2 Tbsp. Smoky Mountain liquid sweetener	2 Tbsp. lemon juice
	3 Tbsp. cornstarch
3 Tbsp. butter	1/2 cup Brown Sugar Twin
1 tsp. cinnamon	Prepared pie crust

Bring juice, liquid sweetener, butter and spices to a boil. Mix lemon juice with apples, then add apples to juice mixture and cook apples until barely tender. Lift apples out of juice with a slotted spoon.

Mix cornstarch with Brown Sugar Twin and stir into boiling juice mixture. Cook until thick. Pour over apples and cool before pouring into prepared (unbaked) pie crust. Bake at 400° 30 to 40 minutes, until golden brown.

▲ ▲ ▲

Blackberry cobbler

This recipe from Nancy Cannon of Knoxville is for use when blackberries are in season.

3 cups self-rising flour
1 1/2 cups solid vegetable shortening
1/3 cup water
About 12 cups blackberries
3 cups sugar
1 stick butter

Combine flour and shortening. Add water and toss until dough makes a ball. Chill.

Divide dough in half with a little more dough in the half for the bottom layer. Roll out dough thinly for bottom layer, enough to cover bottom of 9-by-13-inch dish or pan and up the sides.

Wash well and pick over blackberries. Drain on paper towels and place in bowl. Add sugar and spoon into unbaked crust. Dot top with butter. Roll out remaining dough for top crust. Place over berries and cut vents for steam to escape. Bake at 325° for 1 hour or until brown.

▲ ▲ ▲

Cranberry crunch

Margarette Idol of Corryton sends a recipe for cranberry crunch.

3 cups tart unpeeled apples, chopped
1 (16-oz.) can whole cranberry sauce
2 Tbsp. unsalted margarine, melted
1 cup quick cooking oatmeal
1/3 cup light brown sugar
1/4 cup flour
1/2 cup chopped walnuts

Combine apples and cranberry sauce. Spread in small baking pan (about 8-by-8-inches). Combine remaining ingredients and spread over cranberry-apple mixture. Bake 30 to 40 minutes at 350°. Serve warm.

▲ ▲ ▲
Friendship fruit starter

Roxie Williams, Maryville, sends two recipes for friendship cake, which is made with a fruit starter. Friendship cakes are called such because you are supposed to share the starter with friends.
One recipe is for cake made "from scratch," and the other uses a mix. She also sends the recipe for starter. She says to start the mixture in a large, clear glass jar with a loose fitting, nonmetallic lid. A wooden or plastic spoon must be used to stir the mixture —never metal.

1 cup pineapple tidbits
1 cup peach slices
1 (8-oz.) jar maraschino cherries
1 1/2 cups sugar
1 pkg. dry yeast (not Rapid Rise)

An 8-cup apothecary jar is best. Drain fruit well. Put ingredients in jar and stir with plastic spoon. Put top on jar and allow contents to ferment in warm place for 2 weeks. Stir once every day, using only a plastic spoon. After 7 days, it is ready to use, but do not add more fruit for two weeks.

Never let the contents get below three cups or the fermentation process will stop.

Every two weeks, add 1 cup sugar and 1 cup of the canned fruits — the first time add 1 cup pineapple; 2 weeks later, 1 cup peaches; 2 weeks later, 1 cup maraschino cherries.

Do not add fruit and sugar more frequently than every two weeks, but you may delay a day or two without disastrous results. Mark a calendar so you will not overextend the time.

Whenever you have 6 cups or more of the fruit, divide portions with at least 3 cups in each. It is best to divide just before adding fruit and sugar. Keep two or three jars going all the time or give some to friends.

Never, never refrigerate the fruit. Store it in a warm place, close to the oven or range top. Never put the lid on tightly or it might explode. You must stir daily to help the sugar dissolve and to prevent fruit from floating.

Serve over vanilla ice cream or orange sherbet. Use it on cake, as a basting agent for baked ham or roast duck, on pancakes and French toast.

See the following page for friendship cake recipes.

▲ ▲ ▲

Friendship cake

1 1/2 cups vegetable oil
2 cups sugar
3 eggs
2 tsp. vanilla
3 cups all-purpose flour
1 tsp. soda
1/4 tsp. salt
1 cup chopped nuts
3 cups friendship fruit, well drained

Blend in mixer the oil and sugar. Add eggs, one at a time, beating well after each. Add vanilla. Sift together the flour, soda and salt and add to first mixture. Mix well. Fold in nuts and fruit. Pour into greased and floured Bundt, tube or 9-by-13-by-2-inch pan. Bake at 325° for 1 1/2 hours or until cake tests done. Cake will not brown, so do not overbake.

▲ ▲ ▲

Friendship cake II

1 (18-oz.) pkg. cake mix
1 small pkg. vanilla pudding
2/3 cup vegetable oil
1 1/2 cups drained friendship fruit
4 eggs
1 cup raisins
1 cup chopped nuts
1 cup coconut

Any kind of cake mix may be used — yellow, spice, lemon.
Combine cake mix, pudding mix, oil and drained fruit in a large bowl. Mix with a spoon. Add eggs and mix. Add raisins, nuts (mixed with a little flour) and coconut. Mix well. Pour into greased and floured Bundt or loaf pan. Bake at 300° for 55 to 65 minutes or until cake tests done.

▲ ▲ ▲
Mincemeat pie

Julia Walker, New Market, sends a favorite holiday recipe, mincemeat pie. It originated with her mother-in-law, Minnie Walker.

1/2 cup sugar
1/2 tsp. salt
1/2 cup corn syrup (dark or dark and light, mixed)
1/4 cup solid shortening
2 eggs
1/2 cup raisins
1/2 cup chopped nuts
1/2 cup mincemeat
1 tsp. vanilla
2 Tbsp. orange juice
1 Tbsp. lemon juice
Pastry for 2-crust pie

In saucepan, combine sugar, salt, corn syrup and shortening. Bring to a boil. Beat eggs and add raisins, nuts, mincemeat, vanilla and fruit juices. Add to hot mixture. Pour into unbaked pie crust and cover with top pastry (pricked with a fork) or lattice strips. Bake at 425° for 30 to 35 minutes.

▲ ▲ ▲
Fried peach pies

Evelyn McKinney, who now lives in Chattanooga, was the first participant in our Recipes and Requests column when it began in 1982. She and her husband, the late A. Wayland McKinney Jr., had lots of visitors to their home during the World's Fair, and she served them her favorite foods. One is her southern fried peach pies, made the easy way with canned biscuits for the dough.

2 pkgs. dried peaches (or apples or apricots)
3 cups cold water
1 cup sugar
2 pkgs. Hungry Jack biscuits

Cover fruit with water in 2-quart pan and soak overnight. Next day cook the fruit until water is absorbed, but do not let it burn. Remove from heat and let set overnight or until completely cold. Add sugar, mix and set aside in refrigerator until needed.

Roll out a biscuit until thin and completely round. Place 2 tablespoons of fruit in center. Fold over and crimp edges with fork to seal. Puncture biscuit three times with fork. Fry in iron skillet with butter and a small amount of clear bacon drippings over medium heat, turning once to brown pie on each side. Or bake, following biscuit instructions. Serve hot. Yield: 20 pies.

▲ ▲ ▲

Too-easy peach cobbler

This recipe has been extremely popular with readers since it appeared in The News-Sentinel. The cobbler uses supermarket-type white bread strips for a crust. The butter and sugar caramelize over the bread strips to make a crispy top.

5 to 6 fresh peaches, peeled, pitted and sliced
1 1/2 cups sugar
2 Tbsp. flour
1 egg
1 stick butter or margarine, melted
5 slices white bread

Preheat oven to 350°. Place fruit in buttered 8-by-8-inch baking dish. Cut crusts from bread slices and cut each slice into five fingers. Place the bread fingers over the fruit.

In a bowl mix sugar, flour, egg and butter. Pour over fruit and bread. Bake for 35 to 45 minutes, until golden. Yield: 5 to 6 servings.

▲ ▲ ▲

Strawberry cobbler

Cecile Jones, Clinton, whose son, Jim Jones, has pick-your-own strawberry farms at Clinton and Lenoir City, makes this cobbler when berries are ripe.

1 qt. (4 or 5 cups) strawberries   2/3 cup solid shortening
1 cup sugar   2 cups self-rising flour
3 Tbsp. cornstarch   1/2 cup buttermilk
1/2 cup water   Butter
1 tsp. fresh lemon juice   Sugar

Wash, cap and slice berries. In separate pan, combine sugar and cornstarch. Add water and strawberries. Heat through. Stir in lemon juice.

Make pastry: Cut the shortening into flour. Add buttermilk, stirring with a fork. This will be a stiff dough. Roll or pat out dough thin. Butter a 2-quart oblong casserole. Put dough in dish, bringing it up on one side so you can fold it over the strawberry filling. Cover dough with strawberry mixture. Fold dough over top. Dot top liberally with butter and sprinkle with sugar. Bake at 400° to 425° for 20 to 25 minutes.

▲ ▲ ▲

Strawberry shortcakes

From White Lily Foods Co. comes this traditional biscuit strawberry shortcake.

2 to 3 cups sliced strawberries, sweetened with 1/4 cup sugar
2 cups self-rising flour
1/4 cup sugar
1/2 cup butter or margarine
1/3 cup half-and-half
1 egg
1 cup whipping cream, whipped
Whole strawberries (optional)

Wash berries. Remove caps, slice and combine with sugar. Set aside. Preheat oven to 425°. Combine flour and sugar. Cut in butter or margarine with a pastry blender until mixture resembles coarse crumbs. Whisk half-and-half and egg together until blended. Stir egg mixture into flour mixture to make a stiff dough, but do not overmix. Turn dough onto a lightly floured surface and knead gently 8 to 10 strokes. Roll or pat dough to 1/2 to 3/4-inch thickness. Cut dough with 2 1/2- to 3-inch biscuit cutter. Place shortcakes 2 to 3 inches apart on ungreased baking sheet. Brush tops lightly with half-and-half. Bake 12 to 15 minutes or until golden brown.

Split shortcakes in half and spoon sweetened strawberries between layers. Replace top layer and spoon on additional sweetened strawberries. Top with whipped cream. Garnish with fresh whole strawberries, if desired. Yield: 6 to 8 shortcakes.

▲ ▲ ▲

Strawberry surprise

This is a wonderful dessert to make with frozen berries.

1 angel food cake
2 Tbsp. cornstarch
1/2 cup sugar
1 cup water
Red food coloring (optional)

2 pkgs. instant vanilla pudding
2 (10-oz.) pkg. frozen strawberries
Whipped cream or topping
Fresh strawberries for garnish

Buy or make an angel food cake. Break it up into bite-size pieces and put in a 9-by-13-inch casserole. Combine cornstarch and sugar in small saucepan. Add water, bring to a boil and cook until thickened and clear. Remove from heat. Add red food coloring, if desired. Pour over cake in dish — it will be a thin layer. Prepare pudding according to directions on package and pour over glaze. Defrost berries and pour over pudding. Top with whipped cream and decorate with large fresh strawberries. Refrigerate until ready to serve.

▲ ▲ ▲

Angel food pie

Mrs. J.R. Pitts, Lenoir City, sends a recipe for a "really good Christmas pie."

2 (9-inch) baked pie shells
1 1/4 cups sugar
1/4 cup cornstarch
Pinch of salt
2 cups boiling water

3 egg whites
1 cup coconut
Coconut (for topping)
Whipped cream

Beat egg whites slightly, slowly add 1/4 cup sugar and beat until stiff, but not dry. Set aside.

In saucepan combine 1 cup sugar, cornstarch, salt and water; cook over high heat, stirring constantly with metal spatula until thickened and clear. Pour hot mixture over egg whites, slowly beating all the time. Mix in the 1 cup coconut. Divide filling into the 2 pie shells. Sprinkle tops generously with additional coconut. Top with whipped cream.

▲ ▲ ▲

Chilled chocolate pie

Betty Jane Lyle in Maryville provides her recipes for the famous lemon (recipe page 159) and chocolate pies that were served at Lyle's Restaurant in downtown Knoxville. Lyle's opened in the '30's and closed in 1973. The recipes are often requested. They do use uncooked egg yolks.

2 eggs
3/4 cup granulated sugar
1 stick margarine, softened
1 tsp. vanilla
2 squares unsweetened chocolate, melted
Graham cracker crust
Whipped cream

Beat 1 egg with sugar and margarine at high speed for 5 minutes (be sure of timing). Add the other egg, vanilla and chocolate and beat for 5 minutes. Pour into graham cracker crust, chill and top with whipped cream.

▲ ▲ ▲

Dark chocolate pie

Ruth Sutton shares a recipe from the Laurel Room at the old Miller's department store on Henley Street, Knoxville.

1 baked 9-inch pastry shell
1/4 cup cornstarch
2/3 cup sugar
1/4 tsp. salt
2 squares unsweetened chocolate
2 cups milk, scalded
3 slightly beaten egg yolks
2 Tbsp. butter or margarine
1/2 tsp. vanilla

Marshmallow meringue:
3 egg whites
1/2 tsp. vanilla
1/4 tsp. cream of tartar
3 Tbsp. sugar
4 Tbsp. marshmallow cream

Mix cornstarch, sugar and salt. Melt chocolate in scalded milk and gradually add sugar mixture. Cook over moderate heat, stirring constantly, until mixture thickens and boils. Cook 2 minutes. Remove from heat. Add small amount to egg yolks. Stir egg yolks into remaining hot mixture. Cook 1 minute more, stirring constantly. Add butter and vanilla. Cool slightly. Pour into baked pie shell. Cool.

To make marshmallow meringue: Beat egg whites until stiff. Add vanilla and cream of tartar. Continue beating and add sugar, 1 tablespoon at a time. Add marshmallow cream, 1 tablespoon at a time, beating until stiff and glossy. Spread over chocolate filling, sealing meringue to edges of pie shell. Bake at 350° for 12 to 15 minutes.

▲ ▲ ▲

German chocolate pie

Pam Shealey of St. John's Lutheran Church, Knoxville, prepares German chocolate pie. The recipe makes enough for two pies.

2 squares unsweetened chocolate
1 stick margarine
3 1/2 cups sugar
1 1/2 tsp. flour
1 Tbsp. cornstarch
2 eggs

1 (12-oz.) can evaporated milk
1 cup chopped nuts
1 tsp. vanilla
1 cup angel flake coconut
2 (9-in.) unbaked pie shells

Melt together the chocolate and margarine. Cool. Mix together the sugar, flour and cornstarch. In a separate bowl, beat together the eggs, milk and vanilla. Add chocolate mixture to milk mixture. Then add sugar mixture. Stir in chopped nuts and coconut. Pour into unbaked pie shells. Bake at 350° for 40 minutes.

▲ ▲ ▲

Milk chocolate pie

Mildred Douglas found one way to her boyfriend's heart many years ago. She made chocolate pie. He married her. She says she has been making the pie since she was 12. She is now in her 60s.

3 Tbsp. cocoa	Meringue:
3 Tbsp. all-purpose flour	4 egg whites
4 egg yolks	1/4 tsp. cream of tartar
1 cup sugar	1/3 cup sugar
3 cups whole milk, scalded	
1 tsp. vanilla	
2 Tbsp. butter	
Graham cracker or regular baked crust	

In top of double boiler, beat together cocoa, flour, egg yolks and sugar. Gradually add scalded milk. Cook over hot water until mixture thickens. Remove from heat and add butter and vanilla. Pour into crust. Top with meringue or whipped topping.

Meringue: In a bowl beat egg whites with cream of tartar until frothy. Add sugar, a little at a time, beating well until meringue holds glossy stiff peaks. Spoon meringue onto warm pie filling and spread, making sure meringue touches all edges of pastry. Bake at 350° 12 to 15 minutes until meringue is lightly browned.

▲ ▲ ▲

No weep meringue

"Weeping meringues" are a problem many readers have asked about. Thelma Otte of Knoxville sends a recipe she has used for over 20 years. She says the recipe makes a very fluffy tender meringue that will not become watery, even on the second day, if you're lucky to have any pie left that long.

1 Tbsp. cornstarch
2 Tbsp. sugar
1/2 cup water
3 egg whites, at room temperature
1/8 tsp. salt
6 Tbsp. sugar

Cook the cornstarch, 2 tablespoons sugar and water in small saucepan until thickened and mixture is clear. Cool. Beat the egg whites and salt until stiff. Fold in cornstarch mixture and continue beating until creamy. Gradually add the 6 tablespoons sugar. Pile meringue on pie, making sure it touches crust all around. Bake at 325° for 20 minutes or until golden brown.

▲ ▲ ▲
Chess pie

Mrs. William Norwood of Knoxville says her chess pie is an old family recipe.

1 stick butter or margarine, melted
1 1/4 cups sugar
1 tsp. cornmeal
1 tsp. flour

1 tsp. vinegar
2 Tbsp. milk
3 eggs
Unbaked pie shell

Combine ingredients, adding eggs last. Pour into unbaked pie crust and bake for 15 minutes at 400°, then at 350° until firm.

▲ ▲ ▲
Coconut chess pie

Mrs. Hoyce Bailey, Kingston, recommends coconut and lemon chess pies.

3 eggs
1 1/2 cups sugar
6 Tbsp. buttermilk
1 tsp. vanilla

1/2 stick margarine, melted
2 Tbsp. cornmeal
3/4 cup coconut
9-inch unbaked pie shell

Cream ingredients until smooth. Pour into unbaked 9-inch pie shell. Bake at 350° for 35 to 40 minutes, or until firm.

▲ ▲ ▲
Lemon chess pie

2 cups sugar
2 Tbsp. flour
2 Tbsp. cornmeal
2 Tbsp. lemon rind
1/4 cup margarine (melted)
1/4 cup milk
1/4 cup lemon juice
4 eggs, beaten
Unbaked pie shell

Mix ingredients well and pour in unbaked pie shell. Bake at 350° for 35 to 40 minutes.

▲ ▲ ▲

S&W chess pie

When a reader requested the chess pie recipe from the old S&W Cafeteria that was on Gay Street in Knoxville, Mrs. W.T. Monday of Knoxville replied. Her brother, the late R.L. Kilgore, was an S&W manager. She has the recipe from the home office in North Carolina.

2 1/4 cups sugar
1 1/2 sticks butter or margarine
1/3 cup cornmeal
4 Tbsp. all-purpose flour
1/4 tsp. salt
1 tsp. nutmeg
1/2 cup egg yolks
1 1/2 cups milk
1 (10-inch) unbaked pie shell

Blend together sugar and butter. Stir in cornmeal, flour, salt and nutmeg. Add egg yolks and mix. Add milk and mix until smooth. Let stand 30 minutes before filling pie shell. Pour into unbaked pie shell that is rimmed up high at the edge. Place in 325° degree oven and bake until done, about 45 minutes.

▲ ▲ ▲

Goo-Goo pie

Jody Frye of Knoxville sends a recipe for Goo-Goo pie. It is a crustless pie.

1/2 cup butter
2 oz. semisweet chocolate
1 cup sugar
1/2 cup flour
2 eggs, beaten
1 tsp. vanilla
1/2 tsp. salt
2 Goo-Goo Clusters candy bars, chopped

Melt butter and chocolate over low heat. Add flour and sugar. Mix with a wooden spoon. Add beaten eggs, vanilla and salt. Stir. Pour into greased pie pan and bake at 325° for 15 to 20 minutes. Sprinkle with chopped Goo-Goo Clusters. Return to oven and bake for 10 minutes. Turn oven off and let pie set for 30 minutes with oven door closed.

▲ ▲ ▲
Jefferson Davis pie

Another favorite from the World's Fair was Jefferson Davis pie made by Rolf Tinner, who was executive chef of the Sunsphere Restaurant. When Doris Pingle of Columbus Grove, Ohio, wrote to request the recipe, the chef provided it.

3 eggs, lightly beaten
1 cup sugar
1 1/2 cups walnuts
2 Tbsp. butter
2 tsp. vanilla
1/4 cup bourbon whiskey
1/2 cup cream
1/8 tsp. salt
1/2 cup honey
1 1/2 cups white seedless raisins
1 (9-inch) unbaked pie shell

Combine all ingredients and pour into unbaked pie shell. Bake for 15 minutes at 350°; reduce heat to 325 and continue baking until pie sets (about 25 to 30 minutes). Serve hot or cold.

▲ ▲ ▲
Jimmy Carter pie

2 (3-oz.) pkgs. cream cheese
3/4 cup confectioners' sugar
1/2 cup peanut butter
2 Tbsp. milk
1 (8-oz.) carton whipped topping
1 baked graham cracker crust

Beat together the cream cheese and sugar thoroughly. Add peanut butter and milk. Blend well. Fold in whipped topping. Pour into baked graham cracker pie crust and chill for several hours.
Serve with additional whipped topping, if desired.

▲ ▲ ▲
Krystal pies

Mrs. Troy Breeden of Seymour saved a clipping from the Jacksonville, Fla.,
Journal with recipes for Krystal old-fashioned ice box pies that had a thin white
icing. She shared a copy of the clipping.
The recipes were obtained from Krystal headquarters at Chattanooga and were
tested by a dietitian at Baptist Medical Center in Jacksonville. The dietitian
converted the original recipes that made a quantity of pies into recipes for
individual ones.
Fillings should be prepared and refrigerated overnight before pouring into a
baked pie shell. Fill to within 1/2 inch of the top of the crust, then top with
whipped cream. Garnish with shredded coconut on the coconut pie; lemon slices
on the lemon pie; and shredded chocolate on the chocolate pie.

Coconut filling:
2 cups milk
1 1/4 cups sugar
6 Tbsp. cornstarch
2 eggs
Dash salt
1/4 tsp. vanilla
1/2 cup coconut

Heat milk in top of double boiler (over hot water) until milk is hot, but
not boiling. Mix sugar, cornstarch and salt in mixer. Add the hot milk. Mix
for 1 minute or until smooth. Add eggs and mix well. Pour mixture back
into top of double boiler. Stir occasionally until mixture begins to coat the
sides of pan, then stir constantly until thick. This will prevent lumping.
Place this mixture in mixer, adding coconut and vanilla and beat until
mixture cools. Chill. Pour into prepared crust.

Lemon filling:
2 cups milk
1 1/4 cups sugar
8 Tbsp. cornstarch
Dash salt
1 egg plus 1 yolk
1/4 tsp. vanilla
2 Tbsp. lemon juice or more, to suit taste
1 Tbsp. lemon peel

Heat milk in top of double boiler (over hot water) until hot, but not
boiling. Mix sugar, cornstarch and salt in mixer. Add the hot milk. Mix for 1
minute or until smooth. Add egg, egg yolk, vanilla and lemon juice. Mix
well. Pour mixture back into top of double boiler. Stir occasionally until

mixture begins to coat the sides of pan, then stir constantly until thick. This will prevent lumping. Let pie cool to room temperature, add lemon peel, beat until smooth. Chill. Pour into prepared crust.

Chocolate filling:
2 cups milk
7 Tbsp. cornstarch
1 1/4 cups sugar
1/4 cup cocoa
1 egg plus 1 yolk
Dash salt
1/4 tsp. vanilla

Heat milk in top of double boiler (over hot water) until hot, but not boiling. Mix sugar, cornstarch, cocoa and salt in mixer. Add the hot milk. Mix for 1 minute or until smooth. Add egg and yolk and mix well. Pour mixture back in top of double boiler. Stir occasionally until mixture begins to coat the sides of pan, then stir constantly until thick to prevent lumping. Place mixture in mixer, add 1/4 teaspoon vanilla and beat until cool. Chill. Pour into prepared pie crust.

▲ ▲ ▲
Lemon ice box pie

This lemon ice box pie, without egg yolks, comes from Irene Monroe, Knoxville.

1 (6-oz.) can frozen lemonade
1 (8-oz.) carton whipped topping
1 can sweetened condensed milk
Graham cracker crust

Thaw lemonade and beat with whipped topping and condensed milk. Pour into graham cracker crust. Chill several hours, until set.

▲ ▲ ▲
Lyle's lemon ice box pie

2 egg yolks
Juice of 2 lemons (or about 1/3 cup)
1 can sweetened condensed milk
Graham cracker crust
Sweetened whipped cream or meringue topping

Beat egg yolks; slowly add lemon juice, then milk. Pour into prepared graham cracker crust. Refrigerate. When ready to serve, top with sweetened whipped cream or with a meringue made from the egg whites.

▲ ▲ ▲

Pecan pie

Phyllis Rainwater, Dandridge, makes this pie.

1 (9-inch) unbaked pastry shell
3/4 cup granulated sugar
1 cup dark corn syrup
3 eggs

1/2 stick butter or margarine
1 tsp. vanilla
1 cup coarsely chopped pecans

Combine sugar and syrup in a saucepan and boil for 2 minutes. Cool slightly. Pour slowly over slightly beaten eggs, stirring with a wooden spoon. Be careful not to overbeat. Add butter or margarine and vanilla.

Pour filling into unbaked crust.

Sprinkle pecans over the top. (Or mix the nuts in with the filling before pouring it into the crust.) Bake at 350° for 50 to 60 minutes. When pecan pie is done, outer edges of filling should be set, center slightly soft.

To freeze, let pie cool. Place in a freezer bag and set it on a cookie tin in freezer. An hour or two before serving, remove from freezer and thaw it at room temperature. When thawed, place in a 325° oven for 15 minutes or until pie is warm.

Light or dark brown sugar and light corn syrup may be used instead of granulated sugar and dark corn syrup.

▲ ▲ ▲

Impossible pumpkin pie

Louise Hodge of Knoxville offers a recipe for no-crust pumpkin pie that uses a commercial baking mix to form its own crust.

3/4 cup sugar
1/2 cup Bisquick baking mix
2 Tbsp. butter or margarine
1 (13-oz.) can evaporated milk
2 eggs
1 can (2 cups) pumpkin
2 1/2 tsp. pumpkin pie spice
2 tsp. vanilla

Heat oven to 350°. Grease 10-inch pie plate. Put ingredients in blender and blend on high. Pour in pie plate. Bake until knife inserted in center comes out clean, 50 to 55 minutes. Garnish with whipped cream, if desired.

▲ ▲ ▲
Sweet potato pie

Ailene Blair, Knoxville, has a favorite recipe for sweet potato pie.

2 lbs. sweet potatoes
3 eggs
1/4 cup butter or margarine
3/4 cup light corn syrup
1/4 cup brown sugar
1 tsp. vanilla extract
1/8 tsp. salt
1 cup whole pecans
1 (9-inch) unbaked pie shell

Cook sweet potatoes in saucepan with water until tender. Drain. Mash sweet potatoes. Measure 1 1/2 cups to use in pie; reserve any remaining for another use. Preheat oven to 350°. Put all ingredients except 1/2 cup pecans into blender container. Cover and process until well mixed. Pour into pie shell and garnish with remaining 1/2 cup pecans. Bake 1 hour or until knife inserted in center comes out clean. Yield: 6 to 8 servings.

Note: This pie is especially good when you substitute pancake syrup that has a maple flavor for the light corn syrup; omit the vanilla.

▲ ▲ ▲
Devil's float

Devil's float is an old-time, popular dessert and when we had a request, we received two versions —one with, one without marshmallows (see following page).

1 1/2 cups sugar
2 cups hot water
1 cup flour
3 Tbsp. cocoa
1 tsp. baking powder

1/4 tsp. salt
2 Tbsp. butter (no substitutes)
1/2 cup milk
1 tsp. vanilla

Combine 1 cup sugar and the hot water and boil 10 minutes. Sift together 1/2 cup sugar and other dry ingredients. Cut in butter until mealy. Add milk, vanilla and mix well. Pour boiling syrup into shallow baking pan. Spoon batter over it. Bake at 350° until cake is done, about 30 minutes. It will float over syrup.

Cake may be inverted on platter, if desired. It may be served hot or cold or with whipped cream.

▲ ▲ ▲

Marshmallow devil's float

1/2 cup sugar	1 cup all-purpose flour
1 1/2 to 2 cups water	1/2 tsp. salt
48 miniature marshmallows	1 tsp. baking powder
2 Tbsp. solid vegetable shortening	3 Tbsp. cocoa
1/2 cup sugar	1/2 cup milk
1 tsp. vanilla	1/3 cup chopped nuts

Cook 1/2 cup sugar and water for 5 minutes. Pour into 2-quart or 8-by-12-inch baking dish. Top with marshmallows. Beat shortening and remaining 1/2 cup sugar. Add vanilla. Add flour, sifted with salt, baking powder and cocoa, alternately with milk. Add nuts. Drop from spoon over marshmallow mixture. Cover with foil or lid. Bake at 350° for 45 minutes. (When done, the syrup will be under the cake, but when served, the syrup is spooned over the cake.)

▲ ▲ ▲

Bread pudding

Pearl McHan of Winston-Salem, N.C., served as cafeteria manager at Carson-Newman College in Jefferson City until her retirement. One of her popular recipes was her bread pudding with caramel sauce. She shares the recipe.

6 cups cubed stale bread	Caramel sauce:
3 cups warm milk	1 cup brown sugar
3 egg yolks or 2 eggs	1/3 cup white corn syrup
1/3 cup sugar	2 Tbsp. butter
1/4 tsp. salt	Few grains of salt
1 tsp. vanilla	1/2 cup evaporated milk or cream
1/2 cup shredded coconut (optional)	1/2 tsp. vanilla
1/3 cup raisins (optional)	

Trim top and bottom crusts off bread and cut bread into 3/4-inch cubes. Scald milk and cool to warm. Combine egg yolks, sugar, salt and vanilla and beat well. Add this mixture to warm milk and mix well. Gently fold in bread cubes, coconut, raisins. Let mixture set 5 to 10 minutes (until bread soaks up liquid mixture). Pour into greased baking dish. Bake at 325° for 1 hour.

To prepare caramel sauce: Mix first four ingredients in saucepan. Stir constantly and boil to the consistency of heavy syrup (about 1 minute). Cool. Slowly stir in the evaporated milk or cream and the vanilla.

▲ ▲ ▲

Bread pudding with whiskey sauce

University of Tennessee football coach John and Mary Lynn Majors made this bread pudding for a March of Dimes Gourmet Gala. The recipe came from Commander's Palace, the famous New Orleans restaurant.

1 cup sugar
1 stick butter, softened
5 eggs, beaten
2 cups heavy cream
Dash of cinnamon
1 Tbsp. vanilla
1/4 cup raisins (soaked in hot water to plump)
12 slices, each 1-inch thick, French bread, fresh or stale

Preheat oven to 350°. In a large bowl blend together the sugar and butter. Add everything but bread; mix. Pour into a 9-inch square pan. Arrange bread slices flat in egg mixture and let stand 5 minutes to soak. Turn bread over and let stand 10 more minutes. Push bread down so most of it is covered by the egg mixture. Do not break the bread.

Set pan in larger pan filled with water that reaches to 1/2-inch from top of pan. Cover with foil. Bake 45 to 50 minutes, uncovering for last 10 minutes to brown. When done, custard should be soft, but not firm. Serve immediately, topped with whiskey sauce, if desired.

Yield: 8 to 12 servings.

Whiskey sauce:
1 cup sugar
1 cup heavy cream
Dash cinnamon
1 Tbsp. unsalted butter
1 tsp. cornstarch
1/4 cup water
1 Tbsp. bourbon
Nutmeg

Combine sugar, cream, cinnamon and butter in saucepan. Bring to boil. Thoroughly mix cornstarch with water and whip into boiling sauce. Cook until sauce is clear. Remove from heat and stir in bourbon. Pour over individual servings of bread pudding. If desired, sprinkle nutmeg over each serving. Yield: 1 1/2 to 2 cups.

▲ ▲ ▲

Grape-Nuts pudding

Arlene Forgione of Clinton sends a recipe for an old-time favorite, Grape-Nuts pudding. She says to be sure the oven is slow to make a firm, smooth custard.

4 eggs
3/4 cup Grape-Nuts cereal
3/4 cup sugar
5 cups milk

Beat eggs until fluffy. Add cereal and let mixture stand 5 minutes. Add sugar and let it set for 3 or 4 minutes more. Stir in milk. Pour into baking dish and bake in very slow oven, 250 to 275°, for 1 1/2 to 2 hours, until set.

▲ ▲ ▲

S&W rice pudding

Jean DeMarcus, Knoxville, sends a recipe for rice pudding that is similar to the pudding served at the old S&W Cafeteria, Knoxville.

1/2 cup uncooked rice
2 1/2 cups boiling water
3/4 tsp. salt
1/2 cup seedless raisins
1/4 stick butter, melted
4 eggs
1 cup sugar
1/2 tsp. salt
1/2 tsp. vanilla
1/2 tsp. lemon extract
2 1/2 cups milk

Lemon sauce:
4 Tbsp. butter
1 1/2 cups sugar
3 Tbsp. cornstarch
3/4 cup cold water
3 egg yolks, slightly beaten
Juice of 2 lemons
1 tsp. grated lemon rind
Pinch of salt

Cook rice in boiling water with salt. When rice is tender, remove from heat, drain and rinse thoroughly. (This is important!)

Soak raisins until plump in hot water to cover (about 5 minutes). Drain. Mix with rice. In a separate bowl, beat together the melted butter, eggs and sugar. Add salt, vanilla and lemon extract. Add milk. Pour over rice and raisins. Pour into 2-quart baking dish and set dish in a pan of hot water. Bake at 350° about 1 hour.

To make lemon sauce: Beat together the butter and sugar. Add cornstarch and mix well. Add cold water and cook over medium heat until clear and slightly thickened. Add a small amount to eggs and stir well. Add eggs to sugar mixture and cook, stirring constantly, until hot and thick. Remove from heat and add lemon juice and rind and salt.

▲ ▲ ▲

* Sugar-free ice cream

Betsy Bohannon, University of Tennessee Medical Center clinical dietitian and certified diabetes educator, sends a recipe for sugar-free ice cream in answer to a reader's request.

2 eggs
Liquid sweetener equivalent to 6 Tbsp. sugar
1/8 tsp. salt
2 cups milk, scalded
1 tsp. vanilla
1 1/2 cups evaporated milk

Beat eggs until lemon-colored. Add sweetener and salt. Place mixture in top of double boiler over simmering-hot water. Heat carefully, adding scalded milk slowly, stirring constantly until the mixture coats a spoon. Cool. Add vanilla and evaporated milk. Chill. Pour mixture into ice cream freezer container and freeze according to manufacturer's instructions.

Tip: Do not allow water in bottom of double boiler to come to a boil. Keep the water barely at simmer. Do not allow the water to touch the bottom of the top pan of the double boiler. Such precautions should prevent mixture from curdling.

Experiment by adding fruits to the ice cream — peaches, bananas. But diabetics will have to figure in a fruit exchange.

▲ ▲ ▲

Lemon or lime buttermilk sherbet

Shirley McMurtrie, Maynardville, writes: "Something about buttermilk makes an excellent sherbet." She shares this recipe.

1/4 cup sugar
1/8 tsp. salt
1 tsp. grated lemon or lime peel
1/2 cup light corn syrup
1 1/2 cups buttermilk
Drop of lemon or green food coloring (optional)

Stir together all ingredients. Pour into 8-by-8-by-2-inch metal baking pan or in 2 ice cube trays. Cover tightly with plastic wrap and freeze about 2 hours or until mixture is partially frozen. Turn into chilled bowl and beat until fluffy. Return to pan. Cover airtight and freeze until firm, about 2 hours or overnight. Cut in squares. Yield: 6 servings.

▲ ▲ ▲

Buttermilk sherbet

This version of buttermilk sherbet is from Mrs. Bob Cusick, Lenoir City. She says it was a favorite when she was growing up. Her mother, the late Lillie B. Crass, prepared it often in the hot summer months and Mrs. Cusick enjoyed it even though she doesn't like buttermilk.

1 (3-oz.) package lemon gelatin
1 cup boiling water
1 cup sugar
1 cup buttermilk
1 (20-oz.) can crushed pineapple

Dissolve gelatin in water. Add sugar and stir until dissolved. Add buttermilk and pineapple (juice and all). Pour into two freezer trays or an aluminum pan. Freeze until mushy. Beat, then freeze again.

▲ ▲ ▲

Hot fudge sauce

Carolyn Broady, Pigeon Forge, sends a recipe for hot fudge sauce that she says is the closest she has found to the ice cream parlor type.

1 (6-oz.) pkg. semisweet chocolate morsels
1 stick margarine
1 to 2 cups sifted confectioners' sugar (according to taste)
1 1/3 cups evaporated milk
1 tsp. vanilla

Melt chocolate morsels and margarine over low heat, stirring occasionally. Add, stirring to blend well, the sugar and milk. Bring to boil and cook about 8 minutes, stirring constantly. Add vanilla. Serve warm over ice cream or cake. Refrigerate leftover sauce and reheat as needed.
Yield: 2 2/3 cups.

▲ ▲ ▲

Sopaipillas or bunuelos

Nancy Bissell, New Market, sends a recipe for sopaipillas. She had the dessert when visiting in a Mexican home. The hostess shared the recipe with her.

2 1/2 cups all-purpose flour	Sauce:
1/2 tsp. baking powder	1 1/4 cups brown sugar
1 tsp. salt	1 small stick cinnamon
2 eggs	2 cups water
1/4 cup butter, melted	1/2 cup wine (optional)
3/4 cup milk or water	1/2 cup raisins (optional)

Sift dry ingredients together. Combine beaten eggs, butter and milk and as much flour as it will absorb. Knead as for tortillas, only make balls the size of walnuts. Press thin or roll as thin as possible. Fry on both sides in deep fat until a delicate golden brown. Serve with brown sugar sauce or honey.

▲ ▲ ▲

Tea cakes

Blanche Franks, Knoxville, sends a recipe from a 1959 issue of "The Progressive Farmer" for a reader who wanted a recipe for old-fashioned tea cakes.

1 cup shortening
3 cups sugar
2 eggs, slightly beaten
1 cup milk
1 tsp. vanilla
1/2 tsp. nutmeg
1 cup buttermilk
1 1/2 tsp. soda
8 to 10 cups flour, or enough to make a soft dough

Cream shortening and sugar. Add eggs, milk, vanilla and nutmeg and stir well. Mix buttermilk and soda and then add to the mixture. Mix in enough flour to make a soft dough. Roll thin, cut into strips lengthwise, then across to make squares and rectangles. Place in greased pans and bake at 400° for 10 to 12 minutes. Yield: 10 to 12 dozen tea cakes.

Candies and cookies

▲ ▲ ▲

Candies and cookies

▲ ▲ ▲
Bourbon balls

From Vera Balloch, Greenville, S.C., comes a recipe for bourbon balls. Some people call them spirit balls because other spirits may be used, she says. "The first time I used rum, but we prefer bourbon."

2 cups graham cracker crumbs
2 Tbsp. cocoa
1 cup confectioners' sugar
1/8 tsp. salt
1 cup finely chopped nutmeats
1 1/2 Tbsp. honey or syrup
1/4 cup bourbon (rum or brandy)
Confectioners' sugar

Place the crumbs in a mixing bowl, add cocoa, 1 cup sugar, salt, chopped nuts. Mix thoroughly. Add honey and bourbon. Mix well. Shape into balls about 1 inch in diameter with hands dusted with confectioners' sugar. If mixture is too dry to hold together, add a bit more liquid. Roll balls in confectioners' sugar. Place in a tin box for about 12 hours before serving or store in a covered container. Yield: 40 to 45 balls.

▲ ▲ ▲
Butter mints

Uncooked butter mints are a specialty of Louise Cannon of Loudon. The recipe is one she created herself. The mints may be formed into a particular design with a cake decorating kit or into a small ball with the hands.

3 Tbsp. soft butter
1/4 cup cream
1/4 tsp. salt
1 tsp. vanilla
1 tsp. peppermint flavoring
1 tsp. butter flavoring
1 lb. confectioners' sugar (sifted)

Mix all ingredients. Color as desired. Make into balls; press down or use cake decorating kit and make into desired shapes on waxed paper. Let dry in the open for at least 1 day. Yield: about 50 mints depending on size.

▲▲▲
Chocolate drops

2 (16 oz.) pkgs. confectioners' sugar
1 1/2 cups sweetened condensed milk
1/2 cup butter, melted
1 tsp. vanilla extract
2 cups chopped pecans
1 cup coconut
1 (12 oz.) pkg. semisweet chocolate morsels
3 Tbsp. shortening

Combine confectioners' sugar, sweetened condensed milk, butter and vanilla. Stir in chopped pecans and coconut. Form into balls. Combine in top of double boiler the chocolate morsels and shortening. Bring water to boil and heat chocolate until it melts. Dip balls in chocolate. Store in refrigerator.

▲▲▲
Church windows

Mildred Vincent of Athens contributes this recipe that is popular in her home.

1 (12 oz.) pkg. semisweet chocolate morsels
1/2 cup butter or margarine
1 (10 oz.) pkg. multicolored miniature marshmallows
1 cup finely chopped pecans
Flaked coconut

Melt chocolate and butter over low heat; cool. Add marshmallows and nuts to chocolate mixture. Shape into 2 rolls, 1 1/2 to 2 inches in diameter. Roll each in coconut. Refrigerate. When rolls are thoroughly chilled, slice into 1/2 inch slices. Makes about 3 dozen.

▲ ▲ ▲

Copycat Goo-Goo Clusters

Rebecca Cook, Knoxville, sends a recipe for making candy like Goo-Goo Clusters. She uses a variety of nuts in the candies. Her favorites are black walnuts or pecans. The peanuts and marshmallows were added after a family member developed a taste for regular Goo-Goo Clusters.

1 pkg. caramels
3 Tbsp. milk
1 cup nuts (pecans, black walnuts or unsalted roasted peanuts)
1 cup miniature marshmallows (optional)
1 (12 oz.) pkg. semisweet chocolate morsels
1/4 bar paraffin

Place unwrapped caramels and milk in the top of a double boiler and heat over boiling water until melted, stirring occasionally. After all the caramels have melted, remove from heat and beat until smooth, about 1 minute.

Stir the nuts into the caramel mixture. Add marshmallows, if desired. Drop by spoonfuls onto buttered waxed paper. Allow the caramel-nut centers to rest until set.

In top of double boiler over boiling water, combine chocolate morsels and paraffin. Heat until melted, stirring occasionally. After all have melted, stir until smooth. Remove from heat. Dip caramel-nut centers into the chocolate. Place on unbuttered waxed paper. If the chocolate starts to harden before all have been dipped, it may be reheated.

Note: Candy coating can be used in place of chocolate morsels and paraffin. Follow package directions.

▲ ▲ ▲

Millionaires

From Mildred Vincent, Athens.

1 (14 oz.) pkg. caramels
3 to 4 Tbsp. milk
2 cups pecan pieces
Butter or margarine
1/4 bar paraffin
1 (12 oz.) pkg. semisweet chocolate morsels

Melt caramels in milk over low heat; add pecans. Drop by teaspoon onto buttered, waxed paper. Chill. Melt paraffin and chocolate morsels in a heavy saucepan over low heat or in top of double boiler over boiling water. Dip candy into chocolate and return to waxed paper. Chill. Yield: About 3 dozen.

▲ ▲ ▲

Mounds candy

3 sticks butter or margarine
2 (1 lb.) pkgs. confectioners' sugar
2 cans sweetened condensed milk
2 (14 oz.) bags coconut
2 (12 oz.) pkgs. semisweet chocolate morsels
1 square paraffin

Melt butter in milk over low heat, stirring all the time. Remove from heat and stir sugar and coconut into milk mixture. This mixture is very soft and more sifted confectioners' sugar may be added to make a firmer mixture.

Spoon onto buttered cookie sheet. Cut coconut mixture into 1-inch pieces. Refrigerate for 2 hours (or freeze 30 minutes).

Melt chocolate morsels and paraffin over low heat or in top of double boiler over boiling water until melted and thin. Dip coconut pieces into chocolate mixture. Harden by placing candy on foil and refrigerating.

Remove from cookie sheet to a box (with lid) with a fork or small spatula to keep from spotting. Crumble plastic wrap between layers. Cover with plastic and place lid on box. Refrigerate.

Variation: Add 2 1/2 cups chopped pecans and a tablespoon of vanilla.

▲ ▲ ▲

Pecan crunch

Pecan crunch is easy to make and almost no-fail, Helen McCrary of Fall Branch says. Walnuts or almonds could be substituted for the pecans. The candy is chocolate coated on both sides.

1/2 lb. butter
1 cup superfine granulated sugar
1 Tbsp. white corn syrup
1/4 tsp. salt
3 Tbsp. water
1 cup chopped pecans
3 squares semisweet chocolate

Melt chocolate over hot (not boiling) water until soft enough to spread with pastry brush. In separate saucepan, melt butter, add sugar and stir until dissolved. Add corn syrup, salt and water and cook to 290° stirring all the time. Remove from heat and add chopped pecans. Return to heat, and cook 3 minutes, stirring constantly.

Pour onto cold marble slab or cold cookie sheet. Using pastry brush spread chocolate over candy and sprinkle with chopped nuts. Turn candy over and brush other side with chocolate and sprinkle with nuts. When chocolate sets (candy will be completely cooled), break into pieces with fingers. Store in covered container.

▲ ▲ ▲
Cream (pull) candy

Helen McCrary of Fall Branch gives several suggestions for candymaking. She
agrees with the old rule: Try not to make candy on rainy days.
Do not stir cream candy while it is cooking or when pouring it from the pan, she
cautions. Because she has had trouble with the candy crystallizing recently, she
purchased superfine sugar and new cans of baking powder. She always uses a
candy thermometer, and suggests that homemakers occasionally check theirs by
testing it in boiling water. It should register 212° at boiling.
A homemade baking powder mixture must be used in this recipe. It is made by
sifting together 2 tablespoons cream of tartar, 1 tablespoon baking soda and 1
tablespoon cornstarch. Store in airtight container.
Use pure flavorings, she suggests. She purchases peppermint and almond
flavorings at the drug store. And store candy in airtight containers.

3 cups superfine granulated sugar
2 tsp. homemade baking powder
1/2 tsp. salt
1 cup water
1/4 lb. butter (no substitute)

Mix sugar, baking powder and salt in heavy medium-size saucepan.
Then add water and butter. Wrap wet paper towel around knife and clean
around side of pan to remove crystals. Cook all ingredients over medium
heat to 260° using a lid during first part of cooking to steam down crystals.
Do not stir. If any crystals form during cooking, wipe sides again with knife
wrapped in wet paper towel.

Pour onto a cold buttered marble slab (18 by 18 inches) or on a cold
porcelain buttered platter. Let candy drip out of pan and do not use spoon.
Choose one of the following food color and flavoring combinations and
drop into candy. It will mix in as candy is pulled:

5 drops peppermint and 6 drops green food color
1/4 tsp. pure almond flavoring and 6 drops red color
1 1/2 tsp. pure lemon flavoring and 8 drops yellow color
1 tsp. pure vanilla and no color

Work around outer edge of candy with table knife turning edges toward
center. When cool enough to handle, pick up with buttered hands and pull.
Turn ends over into center so that all parts will be evenly pulled. Pull into
long ropes (do not twist). Pull until the candy becomes non-glossy, creamy
and light. It makes a 2- to 4-foot strip.

Place strip on clean counter top and immediately cut into pieces with
scissors. Cut small for party size, or in 1-inch lengths. Place in tightly
covered container in warm place to soften. Usually takes 3 or 4 days for
candy to ripen and become soft and creamy. Yield: 1 1/2 lbs.

▲ ▲ ▲
English toffee

Following is an English toffee recipe from Anne Lambert of Knoxville.

1 cup butter (2 sticks)
1 cup sugar
2 Tbsp. water
1 Tbsp. light corn syrup
3/4 cup broken nuts (pecans or almonds)
4 oz. semisweet chocolate morsels or squares, melted
1/4 cup very finely chopped nuts

Melt butter. Add sugar. Bring to slow boil, then add water and corn syrup. Stir well. Turn heat to low and cook to hard-crack stage, 290° on candy thermometer. Remove from heat and add the broken nuts at once. Pour into lightly buttered 9-by-13-inch pan. Quickly spread with spatula. When cool, spread chocolate over top and sprinkle with the 1/4 cup finely chopped nuts. Break in pieces and serve. Yield: 1 1/4 lbs. Note: It's best to make this on a sunny day.

▲ ▲ ▲
Amaretto fudge

Ann Cox, Nashville, offers a recipe for amaretto fudge to be made in the microwave oven.

1 (16-oz.) pkg. semisweet chocolate morsels
1 (14-oz.) can sweetened condensed milk
1/4 cup amaretto
1 tsp. almond extract
1 (3/4-oz.) pkg. slivered or sliced almonds

Combine chocolate morsels and milk in mixing bowl and cover loosely. Cook for 3 minutes in microwave on high. Remove from microwave and stir until mixture is smooth. Stir in amaretto and almond extract. Grease 8-by-8 inch square pan and sprinkle with almonds to cover bottom of pan. Pour mixture in pan and let set up. (It will speed up process to chill it in refrigerator.) Cut in 1-inch squares. Yield: 64 pieces.

▲ ▲ ▲

Butterscotch fudge

Jean Crosby-Harville, Morristown, makes a butterscotch fudge that her friends love.

3 cups granulated sugar
1 stick margarine
1 (5-oz) can evaporated milk
1 small pkg. (1 cup) butterscotch morsels
1 (7-oz.) jar marshmallow cream
1 1/2 tsp. vanilla
1 cup coconut

Mix sugar, margarine and milk and place in saucepan over medium heat, stirring constantly. (Harville cooks it in a porcelain type pan; it will brown a little on the bottom, but that doesn't hurt the flavor or the color, she says.)

Cook until mixture comes to a soft ball stage, 236°. Remove from heat and add butterscotch morsels, marshmallow cream, vanilla and coconut. Stir together, mixing well. Mixture will be shiny. Pour into 13-by-9-by-2-inch buttered pan. Cool; then cut into pieces.

▲ ▲ ▲

Chocolate fudge

Marie Burnett, Knoxville, prepares this fudge to give to friends.

5 cups granulated sugar
1 (13-oz.) can evaporated milk
3 sticks whipped margarine
18 oz. (1 large, 1 small pkg.) chocolate morsels
1 (7-oz.) jar marshmallow cream
1 cup chopped pecans

Mix together sugar, evaporated milk and margarine. Bring to boil over medium heat, stirring constantly so mixture won't stick. Boil for 8 minutes. Add chocolate morsels and marshmallow cream. Mix well and add chopped pecans. Pour into two buttered baking dishes and let set until it cools. Cut into pieces.

▲ ▲ ▲

Microwave fudge

3 cups sugar
3/4 cup margarine
1 (5-oz.) can evaporated milk
1 (12 oz.) pkg. chocolate morsels
7 oz. jar marshmallow cream
1 cup chopped nuts
1 tsp. vanilla

Microwave margarine on high 1 minute or until melted. Add sugar and milk, mix well. Microwave on high 5 minutes or until boiling, stir after 3 minutes. Mix well, scrape bowl. Microwave 5 1/2 minutes, stirring after 3. Gradually stir in chocolate until melted. Stir in other ingredients. Spread in greased pan. Let cool; cut in squares. Yield: 3 pounds.

▲ ▲ ▲

Million dollar fudge

Evelyn McKinney, now of Chattanooga and formerly of Knoxville, offers Mamie Eisenhower's million dollar fudge, a recipe that's been a favorite with News-Sentinel readers.

4 1/2 cups sugar
Pinch of salt
2 Tbsp. butter
1 (13-oz.) can evaporated milk
1 (12-oz.) pkg. semisweet chocolate morsels
12 oz. German sweet chocolate
2 (7-oz.) jars marshmallow cream
2 cups chopped nuts

Combine sugar, salt, butter, evaporated milk in saucepan and boil 6 minutes. Combine in a large bowl the chocolate morsels, German sweet chocolate, marshmallow cream and nuts. Pour boiling syrup over ingredients in bowl; beat until chocolate is all melted and pour into flat pan. Let stand a few hours before cutting. Store in tin box.

▲ ▲ ▲

Peanut butter fudge

Bea Lay of Rockwood says her fudge recipe is a "no-fail."

2 cups sugar
1/4 cup light corn syrup
1/2 cup milk
1/4 tsp. salt
2 Tbsp. butter or margarine
1 tsp. vanilla
1 cup creamy peanut butter
1/2 cup chopped peanuts, optional

Combine sugar, corn syrup, milk, and salt in a medium-sized saucepan. Cook over low heat, stirring constantly until sugar dissolves. Cover pan for 1 minute to allow steam to wash down the sugar crystals that cling to side of pan, or wipe down the crystals with a damp cloth. Uncover pan; insert candy thermometer. Cook without stirring until candy thermometer reaches 236°, soft ball stage when a bit of syrup dropped into cold water forms a ball and flattens on removal from water.

Remove candy from heat. Add butter. Cool syrup until lukewarm, 110°. Add vanilla, peanut butter (and chopped peanuts, if desired.) Beat until candy begins to thicken and loses its high gloss. Turn immediately into buttered 8-by-8-by-2-inch pan. Score with sharp knife into small squares. When completely cool, cut squares all the way through. Store 2 to 3 weeks in tightly covered container with foil or plastic wrap between layers.

▲ ▲ ▲

Peanut butter fudge II

Nita Noe of Knoxville sends a peanut butter fudge recipe.

3 cups sugar
3/4 cup margarine
1 (5-oz.) can evaporated milk
1 (18 oz.) jar chunky peanut butter
1 (7 oz.) jar marshmallow cream

Combine sugar, margarine and milk; stir until mixture boils. Boil 5 minutes. Remove from heat and stir in peanut butter and marshmallow cream. Stir until smooth. Pour into 9-by-13-by-2 inch pan. Cool. Cut into small squares.

▲ ▲ ▲

Creamy peanut butter fudge

2 cups sugar
1/4 tsp. salt
2 Tbsp. corn syrup
1 (5-oz.) can evaporated milk
1 tsp. vanilla
1/2 cup creamy peanut butter

Mix sugar, salt, syrup and milk in heavy pan. Bring to boil slowly. Cook until small amount forms soft ball in cold water, 236° on candy thermometer. Remove from heat. Add peanut butter and vanilla. Do not stir. Cook to lukewarm. Beat just until creamy, when it is losing its gloss and is beginning to hold shape. Pour into greased 8-by-8-inch pan. Cool.

▲ ▲ ▲

Pumpkin pie fudge

Pauletta Johnson, Englewood, sends this recipe that calls for a couple of unusual items — orange chocolate coating and butterscotch chocolate. Both are available at Sugarbakers Cake and Candy Supplies in Knoxville.

12 oz. orange chocolate
4 oz. butterscotch chocolate
3/4 tsp. pumpkin pie spice
1/8 tsp. nutmeg flavoring (concentrated)
1/8 tsp. cinnamon flavoring (concentrated)
1 can sweetened condensed milk

Melt chocolate coatings over hot water. Add spices and sweetened condensed milk. Mix well. Pour into 8-by-8 inch buttered pan. Chill for 1/2 hour and cut. If desired, decorate with miniature pumpkin candies.

▲ ▲ ▲

Velveeta cheese fudge

1 lb. margarine
1 lb. Velveeta cheese
4 lbs. confectioners' sugar
1 cup cocoa
1 Tbsp. vanilla
Chopped nuts (optional)

In saucepan, melt margarine and cheese. Sift together sugar and cocoa, adding sugar 1 pound at a time. Very gradually add dry ingredients to melted mixture, stirring well. Add vanilla and nuts. Spread evenly in a greased 9-by-13-inch pan. Cool and cut in pieces. Yield: 6 1/2 lbs.

▲ ▲ ▲
Buckeyes

Debbee Peoples, New Market, offers this recipe.

2 cups chunky peanut butter
1 stick softened margarine
2 cups confectioners' sugar
3 cups Rice Krispies

6 oz. chocolate morsels
1/3 bar paraffin

Combine first 4 ingredients in large bowl. Mix well and chill. Form into walnut size balls and chill. Melt chocolate morsels and paraffin in saucepan. Dip balls in chocolate mixture. Place on wax paper until firm.

▲ ▲ ▲
Peanut butter balls

Berniece Shamblin, Etowah, provides this.

1 can sweetened condensed milk
2 boxes confectioners' sugar
2 sticks margarine, room temp.
Peanut butter, to taste

Chocolate coating:
1/3 bar paraffin
12 oz. chocolate morsels

Combine milk, sugar, margarine and peanut butter. Chill. Roll into balls. Melt chocolate coating ingredients together in double boiler. Dip peanut butter balls in chocolate coating.

▲ ▲ ▲
Peanut butter roll candy

A cooked potato is one of the ingredients of Louise Cannon's candy.

1 medium sized potato
1/2 stick margarine
1/4 cup evaporated milk
1 tsp. vanilla

Dash salt
Confectioners' sugar
Peanut butter

Boil potato until done. While still hot, mash thoroughly. Add margarine, milk, vanilla and salt. Add confectioners' sugar, small amounts at a time, until potato and confectioners' sugar mixture is at a rolled dough stage. Amount of confectioners' sugar depends on size of potato. It may take two or three boxes.
Roll out to 1/4-inch thickness on cloth which has been sprinkled with sifted confectioners' sugar. Spread evenly with soft peanut butter and roll up. Let set about 30 minutes. Slice into 1/4- or 1/2-inch pieces. Serve cold.

▲ ▲ ▲

Penuche

Margaret Craig Schmidt, Crossville, contributes a recipe for "perfect" penuche.

1 lb. brown sugar
1 stick butter (no substitute)
1 cup whipping cream
1 cup nuts
1 tsp. vanilla

Boil first 3 ingredients, stirring almost constantly until a drop in cold water forms a soft ball. Remove from heat and add nuts and vanilla. Beat mixture until it begins to thicken. Pour in 9-by-9-inch lightly-greased pan or miniature candy foil papers. Candy will improve in creaminess when it stands 2 or 3 days.

▲ ▲ ▲

Strawberry candy

Mildred Morgan of Knoxville shares this recipe.

2 cups chopped pecans
2 small pkgs. strawberry gelatin
1 can sweetened condensed milk
1 large can angel flake coconut
1 tsp. almond or vanilla flavoring
Red colored granulated sugar
Green colored granulated sugar
80 almond slivers
Green food coloring

Mix chopped pecans, gelatin, condensed milk, coconut and flavoring and place in refrigerator 1 hour or overnight. Place slivered almonds in jar with green food coloring. Shake well to coat. Shape gelatin mixture into strawberries; roll in red sugar. Dip stem end in green sugar; insert almond for stem. Yield: 80 candies.

▲ ▲ ▲

Chocolate pizza

The mother-daughter combination of Patty and Katie Fowler of Knoxville makes chocolate pizza for cookie exchanges.

1 (12-oz.) pkg. semisweet chocolate morsels
1 lb. white almond bark (white chocolate), divided
2 cups miniature marshmallows
1 cup Rice Krispies
1 (8-oz.) jar red maraschino cherries, halved
2 Tbsp. green maraschino cherries, halved
1/3 cup coconut
1 tsp. oil

Melt chocolate morsels with 14 ounces almond bark in large pan on low heat. Add marshmallows and cereal. Mix well as it all blends and softens. Pour cereal mixture over a large, well-greased, round pizza pan. Top with cherries and sprinkle with coconut.

Melt remaining almond bark in oil over low heat, stirring until smooth. Drizzle over the coconut and cherries. Let set at room temperature 15 minutes. Slice and serve.

▲ ▲ ▲

Congo squares

A 30-year-old recipe from The News-Sentinel is Julia Schriver's contribution. She says the recipe appeared in 1959 and came from Florence D. Austin. Schriver says her family and friends love the cookies.

2/3 cup melted shortening (half butter and half shortening may be used)
1 lb. pkg. light brown sugar
3 eggs
2 3/4 cups sifted all-purpose flour
2 1/2 tsp. baking powder
1/2 tsp. salt
1 cup nuts, broken
1 (12-oz.) pkg. semisweet chocolate morsels

Melt shortening and add sugar. Cool slightly. Add eggs, one at a time, and beat well. Add sifted dry ingredients, nuts and chocolate. Bake in 9-by-13-inch ungreased pan at 350° for 25 to 26 minutes. Do not overbake. Cool and cut into 2-inch squares.

▲ ▲ ▲

Heath Bar cookies

Carol Connor and daughter Mandy of Knoxville make these cookies for Christmas exchanging.

2 sticks butter
3/4 cup brown sugar
Krispy Saltines
1 (12-oz.) pkg. semisweet chocolate morsels
Finely chopped pecans

Melt butter with brown sugar. Bring to a boil and boil 3 minutes. Spray pan or 11-by-16-inch jelly roll pan with vegetable spray. Line pan with Krispy Saltines, placed touching. Pour brown sugar mixture over crackers. Bake at 350° for 5 to 6 minutes. Immediately sprinkle chocolate morsels over top and let melt. Spread chocolate over crackers and top with finely chopped pecans. Chill and cut in squares.

▲ ▲ ▲

Hello Dollys

1 stick margarine
2 cups crushed graham crackers
1 cup butterscotch morsels
1 cup chocolate morsels

1 cup flaked coconut
1 cup chopped walnuts
1 can sweetened condensed milk

Melt margarine in 9-by-13-inch pan. Add in layers the next 5 ingredients in order listed. Do not stir. Pour sweetened condensed milk on top, without stirring or mixing. Bake at 325° for 30 minutes.

▲ ▲ ▲

Praline brownies

This recipe is from Mary Easley, Georgetown, S.C., and comes to us via Edwina Ralston, The News-Sentinel assistant features editor.

1 pkg. Duncan Hines brownie mix with chocolate fudge
3/4 cup light brown sugar
3/4 cup chopped nuts
3 Tbsp. melted margarine

Prepare brownie mix as directed on package and put into 9-by-13-by-2-inch pan. Combine the brown sugar, nuts and melted margarine. Sprinkle over brownie mix. Bake 25 to 30 minutes at 350°. Cool thoroughly. Cut in squares to serve.

▲ ▲ ▲
Scotcheroos

Scotcheroos are another popular bar cookie, and recipes came to us from Marguerite Elder, Ruby Jones and Peggy Beller of Knoxville, Mary Jones of Jefferson City, Bettye Sloan of Madisonville and Sue Deakin of Maryville.

1 cup sugar
1 cup light corn syrup
1 cup crunchy peanut butter
6 cups Rice Krispies
1 (8-oz.) pkg. butterscotch morsels
1 (6-oz.) pkg. semisweet chocolate morsels

Mix sugar and syrup in 4-quart saucepan and bring to a boil, stirring frequently. Remove from heat and add peanut butter and cereal, stirring until well blended. Press mixture into greased 9-by-13-inch pan. Melt butterscotch and chocolate morsels in top of double boiler set over hot water. Spread over cereal mixture. Cool and cut into small squares.

▲ ▲ ▲
Chocolate chip forgotten cookies

If you've forgotten how good forgotten cookies are, try these. News-Sentinel staff writer Cynthia Cummins brought them to the office for sampling. The cookies set in the oven 12 hours — that's why they are called forgotten.

2 egg whites, at room temperature
Dash salt
2/3 cup sugar
1/2 tsp. vanilla extract
1 (6-oz.) pkg. semisweet chocolate morsels
1 cup chopped pecans

Preheat oven to 350°. Beat egg whites in large mixing bowl until foamy. Add salt. Gradually add sugar, 2 tablespoons at a time, beating until stiff peaks form. Fold in vanilla, chocolate morsels and pecans. Drop mixture by heaping teaspoonfuls 2 inches apart onto aluminum foil-lined cookie sheets. Place in oven and immediately turn off heat. Do not open door for at least 12 hours. Gently remove cookies from aluminum foil to wire racks or waxed paper. Store in airtight container. Yield: 3 dozen.

▲ ▲ ▲

Chocolate chip cookies

Ruth Henderson of the Philadelphia community makes wonderful chocolate chip cookies with black walnuts. The recipe makes a great many cookies, so she keeps the dough in the freezer, using as much as she wants at a time. Finding black walnuts can be a problem. Occasionally supermarkets have them or they can be ordered from specialty catalogs. Pecans could be substituted, but the taste will be entirely different.

4 3/4 cups sifted all-purpose flour
2 1/2 tsp. salt
2 1/2 tsp. soda
2/3 cup granulated sugar
1 1/2 cups firmly packed brown sugar
3/4 cup solid vegetable shortening
1 cup very soft (or melted) butter
3 large eggs
4 to 5 tsp. pure vanilla extract
2 (12-oz.) pkgs. semisweet chocolate morsels
1 cup (or more) black walnuts

Sift together the flour, salt and soda. Blend together in a large bowl the granulated sugar, brown sugar, shortening and butter. Add eggs and vanilla and mix well. Stir in flour and blend until dough is well mixed. Add semisweet chocolate morsels and black walnuts.

At this point dough may be frozen in several air-tight plastic containers.

Let dough thaw, if frozen. Roll into balls and place on slightly greased cookie sheet. Bake at 350° for about 10 minutes. Remove cookies from oven when they look not quite done. Yield: about 12 dozen cookies.

▲ ▲ ▲

Orange-coconut balls

Joan Lones of Knoxville sends this version of no-bake orange balls.

1 stick margarine
1 (1-lb.) pkg. confectioners' sugar
1 (6-oz.) can frozen orange juice concentrate
1 (12-oz.) pkg. vanilla wafers, finely crumbled
1 cup finely chopped pecans
2 small cans coconut

Soften margarine and beat, gradually adding sugar. Add frozen orange juice and vanilla wafer crumbs. Add nuts. Shape into small balls. Roll in coconut. Yield: 50 cookies.

▲ ▲ ▲

* Oatmeal cookies

Joan Cohn of Knoxville makes these low cholesterol oatmeal cookies.

5 egg whites, beaten until frothy	1 tsp. salt
1 cup raisins	2 tsp. baking soda
1 tsp. vanilla	1 tsp. cinnamon
1 cup unsalted margarine	2 cups oats
1 cup light brown sugar	1 cup oat bran
1 cup granulated sugar	1/2 cup chopped nuts
2 1/2 cups sifted flour	1 tsp. lemon peel

Combine egg whites, raisins and vanilla. Let stand 1 hour. Thoroughly beat together the margarine and sugars. Sift flour, salt, soda and cinnamon into sugar mixture. Blend well. Blend in egg whites and raisins, oats, oat bran, nuts and lemon peel. Dough will be stiff.

Drop by heaping teaspoonfuls onto ungreased cookie sheet. Bake at 350° for 12 to 15 minutes or until brown.

▲ ▲ ▲

World's best cookies

"The world's best cookies" are really good, and when we printed a request for the recipe, we received responses from R.L. Spetka of Fairfield Glade; Nancy Jones and Irene Monroe, both of Knoxville; Pat Russell of Athens and Sharon Lee of Madisonville.

1 cup butter	1 cup crushed cornflakes
1 cup granulated sugar	1/2 cup coconut
1 cup brown sugar (firmly packed)	1/2 cup chopped pecans
1 egg	3 1/2 cups all-purpose flour
1 tsp. or more vanilla	1 tsp. soda
1 cup vegetable oil	1 tsp. salt (optional)
1 cup quick oats (or regular)	

Beat together butter and sugars until light and fluffy. Add egg and vanilla, mixing well, then add oil, oats, cornflakes, coconut and nuts, stirring well. Next add flour, soda and salt. Mix well and form into balls the size of small walnuts. Place on ungreased cookie sheet. Flatten with a fork dipped in water.

Bake at 325° for 12 to 14 minutes, until lightly brown. Allow to cool for a few minutes before removing cookies from cookie sheets.

Yield: About 8 dozen. Store in airtight container a day or so.

Note: Walnuts may be substituted for pecans.

Miscellaneous

▲▲▲
Miscellaneous

▲ ▲ ▲
Hot cocoa mix

Georgie Diane Lee, Harriman, a mother of two, often keeps her two nieces and a nephew on weekends. Instant hot cocoa mix is an easy beverage that the crew enjoys, she says.

1 (25.6-oz.) pkg. instant dry milk
1 (6-oz.) jar powdered nondairy creamer
2 cups confectioners' sugar
1 (16-oz.) can instant Nestle's chocolate drink mix

Mix ingredients together and store in airtight container in cool place. To serve, mix about 3 teaspoons, or to taste, with hot water.

▲ ▲ ▲
Spiced apple juice

46-oz. jar or can apple juice
1/4 cup firmly packed brown sugar
3 sticks cinnamon
1/2 tsp. whole allspice
1/2 tsp. whole cloves

Pour apple juice into bottom of automatic percolator. Put brown sugar and spices into basket of percolator. Perk as you would coffee.

▲ ▲ ▲
Holiday punch

2 (32-oz.) bottles cranberry juice cocktail
1 (6-oz.) can frozen orange juice concentrate, thawed
1 (6-oz.) can frozen pineapple juice concentrate, thawed
1 (6-oz.) can frozen lemonade concentrate, thawed
2 cups chilled ginger ale

Combine all ingredients at serving time. Pour over ice in punch bowl or serve in a pitcher. Makes 4 1/2 quarts.

▲ ▲ ▲
Percolator punch

Sue Cox prepared this for a Church Street United Methodist Church festival.

4 cups cranapple juice
1 1/2 cups hot water
2 cups unsweetened pineapple juice
1/3 cup brown sugar
1 stick cinnamon, broken into pieces
1 tsp. whole cloves
1/8 tsp. salt

Combine liquids in a percolator. Put brown sugar, cinnamon stick, cloves and salt in percolator basket and let mixture perk. Serve hot.

▲ ▲ ▲
Valentine punch

Chris Bryant, Johnson City, sends a punch recipe.

2 pkgs. cherry Kool-Aid
2 pkgs. strawberry Kool-Aid
2 large cans Hi-C orange drink
2 large cans pineapple juice
1 small bottle lemon juice

Mix water and sugar with Kool-Aid according to package directions. Add orange drink, pineapple juice and lemon juice. Mix well. Chill overnight, if possible. Serve in punch bowl with fresh strawberries for garnish.

▲ ▲ ▲
Lemon iced tea

Felecia Mobley of Knoxville says her Aunt Mae Elam of Springfield has been serving this version of iced tea as long as she can remember. It's perfect for luncheons, she says, and will keep for a week in the refrigerator.

8 tea bags
4 cups boiling water
2 cups sugar
1 small can frozen lemonade concentrate
Water

Steep tea bags in boiling water. Remove tea bags and add sugar and lemonade. Add enough water to make one gallon total. Strain, if desired.

▲ ▲ ▲

Spiced citrus tea mix

Jean Crosby-Harville of Morristown made up this recipe. Change the amount of spices as desired, she suggests.

1 cup Tang
1 cup sugar
1/2 cup decaffeinated Lipton Nutrasweet iced tea mix
1 (6 oz.) pkg. Kool-Aid lemonade mix (sugar sweetened)
1 tub from a package of Crystal Light Fruit Tea, tropical fruit flavor
1/2 tsp. ground cinnamon
1/4 tsp. ground cloves
1/4 tsp. ground allspice

Mix all ingredients well. Store in airtight container. For each serving, use 3 heaping teaspoons per cup of hot water, stirring well.

▲ ▲ ▲

Wine cooler

Karen Childs, formerly of Knoxville, now of Atlanta, sends these two drinks.

10 oz. Spanada or sangria (bottled wine punches)
10 oz. lemon-lime carbonated beverage
10 oz. ginger ale
3 oz. orange juice
1 orange, sliced

Combine all ingredients except orange slices in pitcher. Pour into glasses over ice. Garnish with orange slices. Yield: 4 to 6 servings.

▲ ▲ ▲

Strawberry wine spritzer

1 cup sliced strawberries
2 to 4 Tbsp. sugar
4 mint leaves
1/2 cup white wine

Red food coloring
1 cup club soda, chilled
Strawberries on skewers
Mint sprigs

Combine in blender container the sliced strawberries, sugar, mint and wine. Blend until liquified. Blend in one or two drops of red food coloring. Pour into 2 tall wine glases and pour in enough club soda to fill glass. Garnish with strawberry skewers and mint sprigs. Serve immediately. Yield: 2 servings.

▲ ▲ ▲

Apple butter

Carolyn Wilson Knox sent us a recipe that appeared in a 1988 issue of The News-Sentinel.

1 (64-oz.) jar applesauce (natural, no sugar)
1 tsp. cinnamon
1 cup sugar

Heat applesauce in jar in microwave oven. Pour into roaster and mix in sugar and cinnamon. Bake in conventional oven. Begin at 300° and decrease to 200 to 225° if sauce begins to splatter. Bake at least 8 hours. Pour into sterilized jars.

▲ ▲ ▲

Old-fashioned apple butter

From Mary Chester, Norris, comes this slow cooker recipe for apple butter from "Rival Crockpot Cooking."

12 to 14 apples (preferably Jonathan or Winesap)
2 cups apple juice
Sugar
Cinnamon
Allspice
Cloves
1/2 cup sauterne wine (optional)

Wash, core and quarter apples. Do not peel. Combine apples and apple juice in lightly oiled slow cooker. Cover and cook on low setting for 10 to 18 hours. If using high setting, 2 to 4 hours.

When fruit is tender, put through a food mill to remove peel. Measure cooked fruit and return to cooker.

For each pint of sieved cooked fruit, add 1 cup sugar, 1 teaspoon cinnamon, 1/2 teaspoon allspice and 1/2 teaspoon cloves. Stir well. Cover and cook on high setting for 6 to 8 hours, stirring about every 2 hours. Remove cover after 3 hours to allow fruit and juice to cook down. Add sauterne for the last hour of cooking.

Spoon into hot sterilized jars and process in boiling water bath. Seal. Yield: about 5 (1 1/2-pint) jars.

Note: If you don't have a food mill, put the fruit about 2 cups at a time in a blender and pulse till peel is thoroughly dissolved. Then proceed with recipe as above.

▲ ▲ ▲

Christmas jam

Wilma Nelson, Virginia Bounds, Pollyanna Creekmore and Mrs. Billy Akers Mullican contributed this Knoxville Utilities Board recipe requested by a reader.

1 cup fresh cranberries
1 (10-oz.) pkg. frozen strawberries, thawed
2 cups sugar

Put cranberries in blender. Cover and chop by turning blender on and off, on and off. Empty in saucepan. Add strawberries and bring to a boil. Add sugar and boil 8 to 10 minutes or until thickened. Pour into jelly glasses and seal with paraffin. Yield: 5 (4-oz.) jelly jars.

▲ ▲ ▲

Peach freezer jam

Kathy Johnson, assistant extension agent with the University of Tennessee Agricultural Extension Service, offers this recipe for peach freezer jam.

2 cups finely mashed, fully-ripened peaches
4 cups sugar
1 Tbsp. lemon juice
1 pkg. powdered pectin
3/4 cup water

Combine mashed peaches, sugar and lemon juice. Let stand 30 minutes, stirring occasionally to dissolve the sugar. Stir pectin into water and bring to a boil. Boil rapidly 1 minute, stirring constantly. Remove from heat, add peaches and stir for 2 minutes. Pour into standard (wide-mouth) jelly jars (or plastic freezer containers), leaving 1/2-inch space at top. Seal tightly. Let stand at room temperature until set — about 24 hours. Jam won't be hard-firm, but it will jell. Store in freezer or in refrigerator for a few weeks. Makes 7 (6-oz.) jars or 2 1/2 pints.

▲ ▲ ▲
Hot pepper jelly

Anne Breazeale, Knoxville, shares a recipe that, she said, "was given to me years ago by a Charleston, S.C., friend. If followed, it is a no fail one that will vary with hotness only by the size of hot peppers used."

3 large bell peppers, seeded
12 hot peppers, not seeded
Water
1/3 cup water
3 cups cider vinegar
5 lbs. sugar
2 bottles liquid pectin (Certo)
Red or green food coloring

Place peppers and enough water to cover in blender and pulverize all peppers. Drain well. In large vessel, combine the drained peppers, the 1/3 cup water, cider vinegar and sugar. Bring to boil and boil hard for 5 minutes. Remove and add pectin and coloring. Immediately pour into hot sterilized jars. Leave 1/4-inch head space. Adjust lids. Process 5 minutes in boiling water bath.Yield: 12 to 14 half pints.

If using red peppers, use red food coloring; with green peppers, use green coloring.

▲ ▲ ▲
Hot pepper jelly II

Gladys C. Barkley, Knoxville, obtained the following recipe when she visited her son in Clifton Park, N.Y. "I vary the amount of pepper. Four to six pods of pepper make it HOT. Serve it with meat or on a buttered cracker, or mixed with cream cheese on crackers," she said.

1 cup chopped red hot peppers
1 1/2 cups wine vinegar
6 1/2 cups sugar
1 bottle liquid pectin (Certo)

Grind hot peppers in food chopper. Add to vinegar in saucepan and bring to boil; add sugar and stir until dissolved. Remove from heat. Wait 5 minutes and add liquid pectin. Stir well and pour into small, hot sterilized jars. Seal.

▲ ▲ ▲

Jalapeno pepper jelly

3/4 cup ground green (bell) peppers
1/4 cup seeded and ground jalapeno peppers
5 cups sugar
1 cup apple cider vinegar
2 pouches liquid fruit pectin
Green or red food coloring (optional)

Mix peppers, sugar and vinegar in a large pan or kettle. Bring to a boil. Boil 5 minutes. Cool. Add pectin and boil hard 1 minute, stirring constantly. Stir in food coloring.

Skim off foam and pour into hot clean jars to 1/2-inch of top. Screw lids on firmly. Process in a boiling water bath for 5 minutes. Yield: 5 (8-oz.) jars.

▲ ▲ ▲

No-fail green pepper jelly

June Custead, Loudon, contributes this version.

6 1/2 cups sugar
3/4 cup ground green bell peppers (3 large green, 1 red, plus juice, but measure without juice)
1/4 cup ground red hot pepper
1 1/2 cups vinegar (cider or white)
1 tsp. salt
1 bottle Certo

(Wear rubber gloves when removing seeds from hot peppers. Use hot pepper according to taste.)

Mix sugar, peppers, juice, vinegar and salt. Bring to a hard boil. Boil 5 minutes. Cool 10 minutes. Add Certo, stir well. Skim off foam and let stand 5 minutes. Pour into sterilized jars; leaving 1/4-inch head space. Stir when partially cool to keep pepper from settling to bottom. Seal jars. Yield: about 10 half-pints.

▲ ▲ ▲

Bread and butter pickles

From Kathy Johnson, University of Tennessee Agricultural Extension Service.

4 qts. (about 6 lbs.) medium cucumbers
1 1/2 cups (about 1 lb.) small white onions, sliced
2 large garlic cloves
1/3 cup salt
2 qts. (2 trays) ice, crushed or cubes
4 1/2 cups sugar
1 1/2 tsp. turmeric
1 1/2 tsp. celery seed
2 Tbsp. mustard seed
3 cups white vinegar

Scrub thoroughly, drain and slice unpeeled cucumbers into 1/8-inch to 1/4-inch slices; discard ends. Add onions and garlic.

Add salt and mix thoroughly; cover with ice; let stand 3 hours. Drain thoroughly; remove garlic cloves.

Sterilize canning jars. Combine sugar, spices and vinegar; heat just to boiling. Add drained cucumber and onion slices and heat 5 minutes.

Pack hot pickles loosely into hot pint jars and cover with hot vinegar liquid to 1/2 inch from top. Remove air bubbles. Wipe jar rims. Adjust lids. Process 10 minutes in a boiling water bath. Yield: 7 pints.

Note: Sugar may be reduced to 4 cups if a less sweet pickle is desired.

▲ ▲ ▲

Pickled banana peppers

Mrs. Howell Simery, Oak Ridge, sends a recipe for pickled banana peppers.

2 lbs. yellow banana peppers
Boiling water to cover
2 1/2 cups white vinegar
2 1/2 cups cold water

1 cup granulated sugar
8 cloves garlic
4 tsp. salad oil
2 tsp. salt

Wash peppers. Cut off stem ends only, trimming long peppers to fit pint jars, if necessary. Place peppers in a bowl and cover with boiling water. Let stand 5 minutes. Drain.

Combine vinegar, water and sugar in a saucepan. Heat to boiling and simmer 5 minutes. Pack drained peppers in 4 sterilized, hot pint jars. To each jar add 2 cloves garlic (or to taste), 1 teaspoon oil, 1/2 teaspoon salt. Pour simmering vinegar liquid over peppers to within 1/2-inch of top of jar, making sure vinegar solution covers peppers. Cap each jar at once. Process 10 minutes in boiling water bath. Yield: 4 pints.

▲ ▲ ▲
Pickled green tomatoes

28 medium-size hard, green tomatoes
1 cup pickling lime
1 gallon water
5 lbs. white sugar
3 pints white vinegar
1 tsp. each ground cloves, ginger, allspice, celery seed, mace, cinnamon

Slice tomatoes about 1/4 inch thick. Soak 24 hours in a solution of 1 cup pickling lime and 1 gallon water.

Drain and rinse in fresh water, changing water every hour 4 times. Drain. Mix sugar with white vinegar and spices.

Bring to a boil and pour over tomatoes and let stand overnight. The next day, simmer pickles for 1 hour. Spoon into wide-mouth jars and seal. Process 10 minutes in boiling water bath. Pickles should be chilled before serving.

▲ ▲ ▲
Pickled okra

Sue Cox, Knoxville, shares a recipe for pickled okra.

4 lbs. small tender okra
3/4 cup plain salt
4 cups vinegar
1 cup water
10 pods red or green sweet pepper
10 cloves garlic

Wash okra; pack in 10 hot clean pint jars. Add 1 pepper and 1 garlic clove to each jar. Heat vinegar, water and salt to boiling. If desired, add mustard, celery seed or other seasonings to vinegar mixture. Pour hot mixture over okra and seal. Process in boiling water bath for 5 minutes. Remove jars from canner. Let stand 8 weeks before using.

If desired, add 1 tsp. dill seed to each pint jar.

▲ ▲ ▲
Chowchow

Malla Stephens, Knoxville, sends a favorite recipe for chowchow.

6 red bell peppers
6 green bell peppers
4 lbs. green cabbage
3 lbs. onions
Salt
3 lbs. white sugar
2 tsp. mustard seed
1 tsp. celery seed
1 tsp. turmeric
1 quart cider vinegar

Chop peppers, cabbage and onions. Sprinkle handfuls of salt over vegetables. Stir and let stand 2 hours. Drain. Bring vinegar, sugar and spices to boil. Add chopped vegetables. Simmer 30 minutes. Pack hot into hot sterilized jars. Process 10 minutes; adjust caps. Yield: 8 to 10 pints.

▲ ▲ ▲
Danish green relish

Carol Baumann of Knoxville shares this recipe from an old KUB cookbook, "Pantry Specialties."

30 green tomatoes
4 Tbsp. salt
3 sweet red peppers
1 Tbsp. celery seed
5 large onions

4 Tbsp. dry mustard
3 sweet green peppers
4 cups sugar
5 cups vinegar

Grind tomatoes, peeled onions and seeded peppers in food chopper. Add salt and let stand overnight. Drain liquid and add remaining ingredients to vegetables. Bring to a boil and simmer 15 to 30 minutes. Ladle into hot sterilized jars. Seal at once. Makes 6 pints.

▲ ▲ ▲

American favorite blend

Both Hazel Anderson and Hazel Large send these directions for a salt substitute from an Ask a Dietitian column that appeared in The News-Sentinel.

5 tsp. onion powder (not onion salt)	1 Tbsp. dry mustard
1 Tbsp. garlic powder	1 tsp. thyme
1 Tbsp. paprika	1/2 tsp. pepper

Combine ingredients. Spoon into a clean shaker that has had salt completely removed from it. Add a few grains of uncooked rice to prevent mixture from caking in the shaker.

▲ ▲ ▲

Seasoned salt

Hazel Large also shares a recipe for a copycat version of Crazy Salt. It is a seasoning blend, but it is not a substitute that can be used by those who must omit salt from their diets.

2 1/2 cups kosher salt	2 tsp. paprika
1 tsp. thyme	1/2 tsp. smoked salt
1 1/2 tsp. oregano	1 tsp. curry powder
1 1/2 tsp. garlic powder	1/2 tsp. onion powder
2 tsp. dry mustard	1/4 tsp. dill weed

Combine ingredients. Pour into shaker.

Index

Order blank

Please send me _____ copies of "Louise Durman's Recipes Upon Request."

I have enclosed a check, payable to The Knoxville News-Sentinel, in the amount of $11.95 per copy (includes tax, postage and handling).

Please mail my order to:

Name _____

Address _____

City and State _____ ZIP _____

Mail this form to: **Cookbook, c/o The News-Sentinel, P.O. Box 59038, Knoxville, TN 37950-9038.** Please allow three weeks for delivery.

Order blank

Please send me _____ copies of "Louise Durman's Recipes Upon Request."

I have enclosed a check, payable to The Knoxville News-Sentinel, in the amount of $11.95 per copy (includes tax, postage and handling).

Please mail my order to:

Name _____

Address _____

City and State _____ ZIP _____

Mail this form to: **Cookbook, c/o The News-Sentinel, P.O. Box 59038, Knoxville, TN 37950-9038.** Please allow three weeks for delivery.

Order blank

Please send me _____ copies of "Louise Durman's Recipes Upon Request."

I have enclosed a check, payable to The Knoxville News-Sentinel, in the amount of $11.95 per copy (includes tax, postage and handling).

Please mail my order to:

Name _____

Address _____

City and State _____ ZIP _____

Mail this form to: **Cookbook, c/o The News-Sentinel, P.O. Box 59038, Knoxville, TN 37950-9038.** Please allow three weeks for delivery.